THE DAMN

firefly

AND

SERENITY

TRIVIA BOOK

BY KRISTIN M. BARTON

THE BIG DAMN FIREFLY & SERENITY TRIVIA BOOK
©2012 Kristin M. Barton

Published in the USA by:

BearManor Media
P.O. Box 71426
Albany, Georgia 31708
www.BearManorMedia.com

ISBN-10: 1-59393-681-8 (alk. paper)
ISBN-13: 973-1-59393-681-5 (alk. paper)

Printed in the United States of America.

BOOK DESIGN AND LAYOUT BY VALERIE THOMPSON

TABLE OF CONTENTS

For GINA:
Who is as sweet as KAYLEE,
As tough as ZOE,
As sexy as INARA,
And on occasion, a bit crazy like RIVER.

Introduction
A STORY OF HEROES

When asked in interviews what kind of television shows I like to direct, I usually reply, "That's easy, anything produced and written by Joss Whedon and Tim Minear, because they really let you do the job of directing." It's true. In Hollywood (which is more a State of Mind than a real place), television episodic directors are sometimes marginalized or jokingly referred to as "directing traffic." It's a common practice to pull in the reins so tight on a director that you handicap them, and what they end up actually doing doesn't match the job description. Directors are often blamed as scapegoats when any number of things go awry or amiss. But Joss and Tim are brilliant fellows, and as the creator and showrunner of *Firefly*, they gave me a great story, a talented cast, a fine creative crew, intelligent guidance, and then allowed me to do the job of directing.

I originally started working with Joss Whedon because of my history working with Tim Minear. I've known Tim for many years. We were very young (just out of film school) when we worked on our first feature film, *The Men's Club*, as production assistants. I made less than $200 a week and worked 12-15 hours a day. Tim was so funny and clever and we became good friends. He quickly climbed the ladder as a television writer, while I gained experience in feature films as a script supervisor. I was given my first opportunity as a television director on *ER*, and upon leaving there, it was Tim who gave me my first break by introducing me to the producer of *Angel*, where Tim was the head writer (I've worked on a lot of Tim's shows since then, including *Wonderfalls, The Inside, Drive*, and *Dollhouse*). Tim introduced me to Joss during the final season of *Buffy*, and I was brought on to direct the episode "Storyteller." The episode was well received by Joss, and I was immediately invited back to direct the second to the last *Buffy* episode, "End of Days" (Joss directed the last one himself). After I directed the first *Buffy* for Joss, he was passing me in the office one day, and said "really great episode you directed. It reminded me, *oh, yeah, use the camera to tell the story.*" It stunned me. I've always loved photography and using the camera, but my directing is more influenced by instinct, with an emphasis on communicating well with crew and cast. Joss illuminated something that I was doing unconsciously, and by that, he made me more thoughtful, more focused, and more aware of the effect the camera has as a tool, which can be either forceful or invisible. So when the opportunity to direct and episode of *Firefly* came around, it was a no brainer.

When I first read the script for "Jaynestown," I thought I was damn lucky! It was a Robin Hood tale full of fun, mischief, and merry making. It was a hoot to read (nothing boring!), and the action was there, hand in hand with the comedy. The writer of "Jaynestown" was Ben Edlund (who happens to be a musician), and I was thrilled that he wrote the song, "The Ballad of Jayne" for the episode as well. I was excited that it was a departure from the typical "Western Town" motif that had been established by so many other series. Having a Mud Town would set the episode apart from the rest, and it would be a challenge for the budget since it could turn out horrible and look like nothing, or be something really different. It is a tribute to the talents of the crew that things worked so well. I love that kind of a challenge.

Firefly stands out as the best experience I have had directing for so many reasons. It was exciting to learn of the very different, magical, apocalyptic, yet historically inspired world I was able to immerse myself in. There was limitless potential for a mixture of futuristic and period costumes, sets, and dialogue. The caliber of cast and crew was a high water mark for my experience. On my first day of prep, I walked on the interior of the Serenity set, designed by Carey Meyer, and my jaw dropped. It was brilliant space to work in. No camera angle was a challenge or would look bad. My good friend Loni Peristere did the visual effects, and he is so talented and such a pleasure to work with. I was so lucky to have David Boyd,

Director Marita Grabiak discusses a camera angle while Adam Baldwin takes a water break.
PHOTO COURTESY OF MARITA GRABIAK.

the director of photography and his team, who carried heavy cameras all day long (a big job since most of the shots required hand-helds). A DP can sink you if he is slow, and David was amazing. At the end of the day, it's the director who is responsible for wrapping on time, and time is money. There is big pressure from the studio, but these guys took the ball and ran with it.

We scouted the hot, dry canyons north of Los Angeles and had a look at a location used for the remake of the film *The Time Machine* (2002) as the location for the Mud Town. I wanted to scout there because I'd heard there were stands of bamboo, which were used for a Morlock sequence in the film. Creating a Mud Town out of nothing would really be too expensive for a television budget, so we figured to get good use from the bamboo by creating confusion and obscuring views. One trick I've learned from directing television for so long is that you can film in a small area and still create a sense of a much larger geographic space. You would be surprised to see how small the Mud Town area really was.

Upon visiting the location, the idea was tossed around that on a hot planet the Mudders might just live underground. So as a creative

Marita Grabiak on the "Jaynestown" set with her children.
PHOTO COURTESY OF MARITA GRABIAK.

workable cost-saving measure, all we needed to build were the entrances to underground dwellings. We built one long row of houses, an entrance to the town bar, and the pedestal for the Jayne statue nearby. There was a large dirt pit not too far away, and I had the idea that (if we could afford to pump in water and fill it to a level to create the illusion of depth) it could serve as a mud harvesting pit. I asked the set decorators to come up with machinery, spare parts, anything to make it look a bit like an industrious enterprise which involved a lot of manual labor. I love the look of that pit, and did a long dolly shot to show it off as the Serenity crew was entering the area. There was also a real pond nearby, with great old oak trees as background, which I thought would work well as a location to put Stitch Hessian's jail. Carey's team built some cell blocks and a plank bridge crossing, and it looked amazing.

We shot "Jaynestown" in October of 2001, and during the filming we experienced a record heat, with temperatures reaching over 100 degrees for several days of the shoot. Poor Kevin Gage (the actor who played Stitch)! He was required to wear thick layers of face makeup to create Stitch's look and he was melting under the sun. But despite

Actor Kevin Gage is followed around on set with umbrellas and fans.
PHOTO COURTESY OF MARITA GRABIAK.

the unseasonable heat, Kevin stayed in great spirits (I'm sure it helped that the visual effects makeup team followed him around the set with umbrellas and mini fans). When the sun went down it was a blessing, but there was also a lot of pressure since we had so many pieces of action to shoot. You lose the light early in Canyon country in October, and we barely completed the big fight sequence as the sun disappeared behind a mountain. Later that same day, we lit Stitch's prison pond for a night shoot and the day ended quite wonderfully. On one daunting day at the exterior Mud Town, I broke records with 82 camera setups. Fox studio executives were amazed. Every day was like that on *Firefly*.

The crew was amazing, and there are too many stories to tell, but here's one. The first time I walked onto the Fox lot to inspect the interior set of the Mud Town bar I was so impressed by the level of detail that was present, including the tree roots that intertwined in the walls and ceiling pieces. I noticed the set decorator Dave Koneff was prepping the set by putting sawdust on the floor, and then I saw him pouring bottles of beer right onto the floor. I was mystified and

Adam Baldwin, Kristian Kolodziej, and the head of Jayne's statue.
PHOTO COURTESY OF MARITA GRABIAK.

asked him what he was doing. Dave told me, "I'm adding beer to the sawdust to give the smell of a real bar…I think it will help the actors." I was stunned for a moment and realized that Dave was the first method set decorator I'd ever met. I will never forget that. That was typical of the caliber of everything and everyone on *Firefly*.

Once filming began, I quickly realized what gems I had with the actors. Ensemble casts are generally easier to deal with because not all the pressure is on one actor (which can be a real problem if you have an unhappy diva). But this group was a pleasure. Following *Firefly* I worked with Adam Baldwin again on *The Inside* and Gina Torres again on *Alias*. Nathan Fillion stands out particularly, and I was lucky enough to work with him later on *Buffy*, and then again on *Drive*. Nathan is energetic, funny, supremely good natured, and one of the best guys you could ever meet. They were a good bunch. On a personal note, I had my son Kristian, who was eleven years old at the time, play the Mudder boy who hero worships Jayne throughout the episode.

Firefly was the best kind of job I could imagine; challenging and creative, hard work and rewarding. I went home happy every day and couldn't wait to get to work again the next morning. Everyone collaborated, everyone tried to help everyone else, everyone brought their A game, and when you bring so many talented people together who love the opportunity to do what they do best…well, I think that raised all our games. And that was *Firefly*. In my opinion, anyone who really paid attention to this show and called themselves fans rank as the brightest people in America. I can't wait for the opportunity to work with the likes of Joss, Tim, Nathan, Loni, and all the other cast and crew again. *Firefly* was a dream job, and even after working on other great shows like *Lost* and *Battlestar Galactica*, it ranks as my best experience directing.

Long live great writing and producing.

MARITA GRABIAK
SEPTEMBER 2011

Kristian Kolodziej and Alan Tudyk.
PHOTO COURTESY OF MARITA GRABIAK.

FOREWORD

I remember in 2002 seeing a commercial for a new show coming to Fox that was promoted as the brainchild of Joss Whedon, whom I'd come to learn about earlier that year when I'd been turned on to *Angel* by a friend. I'd since gone back and started catching up on old seasons of *Buffy the Vampire Slayer* and I quickly came to appreciate the artful elegance with which Whedon created his shows and characters. I remember the commercial mentioning space hookers, cowboys in spaceships, and a girl in a box; sounded like a show I'd like. It quickly became one of my favorites.

I also remember in 2002 being frustrated when the show was only sporadically aired and often pre-empted by baseball. Once a string of three episodes would be shown and a story arc would start to develop, *poof!*, gone, only to return unannounced two weeks later. The poorly marketed show and the Friday night timeslot (where TV shows go to die) made my hopes for its survival bleak. But in the aftermath of an early cancellation and with DVD sales that defied expectation, Whedon had truly done the impossible and convinced Universal that his ship and its crew could make it on the big screen. Few dared to truly hope that *Serenity* would ever actually get made, but its release proved what can happen when cast, crew, and fans are all passionate about a project.

Firefly has been part of my life for almost a decade now. And despite its short TV run and *Serenity's* less-than-hoped reception at the box office, the love and admiration I have for that show continues to grow. But the truly remarkable thing is that I'm not the only one. Browncoats around the world have carried on the legacy of the show, and it's a legacy I'm proud to be a part of. This book represents my way of adding to (in some small way) that legacy. My hope is that in reading this book, all of us can rekindle some of the magic we felt the first time we saw Jayne don his iconic hat, Wash play with his dinosaurs, and Zoe refer to the crew as "big damn heroes."

If you Google the term "Firefly and Serenity," your search will yield almost one million web pages of content and information related to the show and film. And while I'm the first person to quickly lose three hours reading *Firefly* articles and looking for new stuff to buy, the questions in this book had to be derived from sources whose accuracy and credibility could be universally agreed upon. Along with the answers in the back, you'll find references detailing exactly where each set of question and answers was taken from.

As I began working on this book, I quickly came upon two challenges that would plague me through its completion. The first of these challenges was how to deal with the word "serenity." In the world Joss created, it refers to so many things. To make reading the questions and answers easier, here's a simple guide you can follow:

Serenity refers to the ship itself.

"Serenity" (in quotes) refers to the episode of the show.

Serenity (italicized) refers to the film.

The second challenge I faced was in determining what type of questions I wanted to ask. I purposely avoided asking questions that I thought were too easy. *What is the name of the captain of Serenity?* If you're reading this book, you're already a fan, so I wanted to challenge you. I wanted to delve into the minutia of the show and see how well you were paying attention. The cast and crew went to great lengths to ensure that the fans would truly enjoy learning about these characters and the process involved with bringing them to life. Have you listened to the DVD commentaries? I hope so, because Jewel and Alan's rendition of the theme song isn't to be missed. Did you look into what was actually being said when the crew spoke Chinese? You need to, because it's probably the only time you'll hear someone on TV say "Holy testicle Tuesday" in any language. My hope is that this gives us all a reason to go back and watch the show we love so much one more time, and maybe introduce a friend, loved one, or total stranger to it as well. Joss created such a rich and textured 'verse for us to enjoy, let's make the most of it and enjoy every bit of it.

KRISTIN M. BARTON
WOODSTOCK, GA
SEPTEMBER 2011

Chapter One
BIG DAMN HEROES

1) What was Mal's rank during the war?

2) Who came up with the idea of throwing the Lassiter into the garbage to get it past security?

3) How many times do we see Simon and Kaylee kiss during the entire run of *Firefly* episodes?

4) Where is Mal hit when Niska's henchman throws a knife at him?

5) What job does Wash tell Mal that he was once fired from?

6) What does Mal tell Simon he will do if anything happens to River during the payroll heist at the beginning of *Serenity*?

7) When Mal and Zoe first meet Wash, Mal states that Wash has earned "a list of recommendations as long as" what?

8) How many switches would Wash hit anytime he did something on the bridge?

9) Besides Mal and Zoe who were on the bridge, who is the first crew member to notice that Wash is not with them once everyone is inside Mr. Universe's complex preparing to fight the Reavers?

10) What does Simon say he was drinking the night he made surgeon, climbed on top of a statue, and started singing?

11) What is Jayne's cut or percent of the profits from jobs the crew does?

12) Who is sent into town to look for the doctor after Book is shot in the episode "Safe"?

13) Who removes the bullet from Simon after Jubal Early shoots him?

14) During their plan to rescue Mal from Niska, Zoe compares what they are doing with throwing a dart and hitting a bull's eye how far away?

15) What does River tell Simon happened to her once she is back on Serenity following the payroll heist and escaping the Reavers?

16) What is Shepherd Book's first name?

17) What is Inara doing when Book brings her supper during his first day on the ship?

18) What does Mal tell Jayne they are stealing from the town just before the Reavers attack at the beginning of *Serenity*?

19) What is the fake captain's name that appears on the official ship's papers that Zoe gives to an Alliance officer when trying to get medical help for Shepherd Book in the episode "Safe"?

20) After the payroll heist when the mule is back on board Serenity, who does Kaylee ask, "Are you okay?"?

21) How does Mal subdue the survivor of the Reaver attack in "Bushwhacked" when he is found hiding behind an air vent?

22) Who upsets Mal during the payroll heist in *Serenity* by yelling out his name?

23) What names do Mal and Zoe give the sheriff of Paradiso while being held after the train job?

24) What does Mal claim he was doing outside Inara's shuttle when he overhears Nandi's call to Inara asking for help?

25) What chores do Jayne, Simon, and Book use to ante up with when they are playing cards?

26) What game are River and Kaylee playing at the end of "Objects in Space"?

27) Who is giving blood to Mal after the shuttles return to Serenity in "Out of Gas"?

28) Whose fake hospital ID badge from the episode "Ariel" identified them as Miles Arixoen?

29) What is Zoe's maiden name?

30) During a flashback at the beginning of "Safe," what does Simon say that River is supposed to be doing instead of playing?

31) After the hospital job on Ariel, what does Mal tell Jayne they used to do to traitors back in the old days?

32) Who is Wash jokingly referring to when he says, "Oh my God, it's grotesque!"?

33) Which member of Serenity's crew originally suggests that they should contact Mr. Universe?

34) What is Inara's last name?

35) What is River doing when Simon finds her after she has disappeared from the store in "Safe?"

36) What did River do that caused Kaylee to chase her around the ship at the beginning of "War Stories?"

37) What is Kaylee's full name?

38) Simon once had a patient name a hamster after him after he did what for her?

39) What is Inara's reason for going to Ariel?

40) What does River claim that the Independents used to cut her and Simon off from Alliance forces when she and Simon are playing together in a flashback?

41) What does Inara say when Kaylee asks, "What's the Companion policy on dating?"

42) According to Mal, what did he once order Zoe not to do that she ended up doing anyway?

43) After making surgeon, Simon and his classmates got naked and climbed on top of a statue of what?

44) What does Simon say it is called when men would be brought in to the ER who had been drugged with a sedative and robbed by women?

45) What holiday does River start talking about when she, Simon, and Jayne are captured by federal marshals on Ariel?

46) What is River drawing pictures of when the crew is all back on Serenity after the hospital robbery on Ariel?

47) In what part of his body is Book shot during the gunfight in "Safe?"

48) What do Simon and Wash both call Mal after Mal claims Kaylee has died in the episode "Serenity"?

49) What does Mal tell Kaylee is the reason he knows the call from Inara in *Serenity* is a trap?

50) Which character does Joss Whedon refer to as "the soul of the ship"?

51) Why does Mal say he wants to take River on the payroll heist at the beginning of *Serenity*?

52) What is the name of the Companion house that Inara belonged to before renting her shuttle on Serenity?

53) After Book is shot in the episode "Safe," who suggests to Mal that they take him to an Alliance medical facility?

54) Who first encounters the survivor of the Reaver attack during the investigation of the derelict transport ship in "Bushwhacked"?

55) When Mal finds Simon in the cargo bay in the episode "Serenity," what does he ask Simon if he forgot?

56) True or False: River is barefoot when she boards the derelict ship attacked by Reavers in "Bushwhacked."

57) Who are the four crew members who watch when Inara calls to ask for Mal's help at the training house in *Serenity*?

58) What does River do in the kitchen while Jayne, Simon, and Book play cards in the episode "Shindig"?

59) Who is the only crew member to put his or her hands up in a gesture of surrender when Alliance soldiers board Serenity in "Bushwhacked?"

60) When negotiating with Mal about renting her shuttle for the first time, what does Inara say that she can bring that none of the other potential renters can?

61) When Inara first rents her shuttle from Mal, what does she say is the foremost thing she would require from him?

62) After Mal returns to Serenity following the duel with Atherton Wing in the episode "Shindig," what does Wash tell Mal he was going to do during the crew's planned rescue?

63) What happens to Simon just before Jayne says, "Saw that comin'"?

64) Where does Mal write the list of medicines they are supposed to steal during the hospital robbery on Ariel?

65) Which crew members does Mal instruct to mount the cannon on top of Serenity after finding the destruction at Haven?

66) Which two female crew members are wearing white at Wash, Book, and Mr. Universe's funeral?

67) What does River do with Tracey's coffin while Jayne and Book are talking?

68) True or False: Inara supported the Indepenents during the war.

69) What was Jayne's cut of the profits with his old crew?

70) Why is Mal upset that River is yelling at the beginning of "Safe"?

71) Simon was in the top what percent of his class at medical school?

72) Whose fake hospital ID badge from the episode "Ariel" identified them as Q. Kumamota?

73) Who tries to help Mal and Zoe carry Tracey's coffin back to Serenity from the post office?

74) How much does Simon spend to see the "alien" with Kaylee?

75) What are Jayne and Book doing when Inara's female client leaves Serenity?

76) Jayne gets shot by a Reaver harpoon in which leg, his right or left?

77) Who finds Saffron looking through the disposal bin for the Lassiter after she has double-crossed the rest of the crew?

78) Who goes up to help Kaylee reprogram the disposal bin in the episode "Trash" after Jayne is knocked unconscious?

79) What does River tell Book will happen before everyone dies from a lack of oxygen after the explosion in the engine room?

80) How many people does Mal personally shoot and kill in the film *Serenity*?

81) Whose fake hospital ID badge from the episode "Ariel" identified them as Kiki LaRue?

82) What part of Zoe does Wash discuss when being interrogated by an Alliance officer in "Bushwhacked"?

83) Which of Mal's ears is cut off while Niska is torturing him, his right or left?

84) In a flashback, how does Zoe kill an Alliance soldier who is sneaking up behind Tracey?

85) Which crew member is knocked unconscious by an explosion in the engine room?

86) What is Jayne doing when River slashes him with a knife?

87) Why does Simon say Zoe will outlive everyone else on the ship after the explosion in the engine room?

88) Which crew member is the first to find Shepherd Book dying after the Alliance attack at Haven?

89) Whose fake hospital ID badge from the episode "Ariel" identified them as Beauma Sclevages?

90) What is physically different about Wash in the flashback to his first meeting with Mal and Zoe in "Out of Gas"?

91) Where does Jayne get shot while completing the train job?

92) What "miracle" does Jayne tell Book he performed that would qualify him for becoming Saint Jayne?

93) After finding Saffron on board claiming to be Mal's wife, Shepherd Book asks which crew member if they have an encyclopedia?

94) How many ranch hands does Mal say helped raise him?

95) What does Mal believe is the real reason Inara passed out during Saffron's take-over of Serenity after Inara admits she didn't trip and hit her head?

96) Who does River say is going to come and take them home after she and Simon have been kidnapped?

97) Despite social and medical advancements, what does young River tell her teacher is the reason the Independents fought so hard against Alliance control?

98) What is Wash's full name?

99) What does Simon compare Jayne to after Jayne tears the infirmary apart?

100) Who are the two people who carry Kaylee into the infirmary after Dobson shoots her?

101) Who does Mal refer to as a "cherry blossom?"

102) Who goes with Inara in her shuttle when the crew abandons Serenity in "Out of Gas"?

103) What does Simon claim is "not exactly the most dignified way" to die?

104) Who is operating the cable that lifts Jayne and the cargo back on to Serenity during the train job?

105) Who tells Simon that Shepherd Book, "ain't a Shepherd"?

106) What nickname does Mal call Simon in the cargo bay when Dobson is pointing a gun at both of them?

107) Where does Mal have a tattoo?

108) What does Jayne say he might do to Simon while Simon is "dead" during the hospital robbery on Ariel?

109) True or False: The order that Shepherd Book follows does not allow him to get married.

110) Why was Simon arrested when his father had to come bail him out of jail?

111) What does Mal tell Zoe she should do if she hasn't heard from him in an hour after he heads to the Training House in *Serenity*?

112) Who is playing guitar while sitting around the campfire after the crew meets up with Shepherd Book at Haven?

113) Who is referred to as "lamby toes," and by whom?

114) On which shoulder does Jayne have a tattoo?

115) How many unarmed men does Mal shoot during the film *Serenity*?

116) What is Jayne doing while Book is "saying a few words" over Tracey's coffin?

117) True or False: At one point, Inara wanted to be a house priestess in a Companion house.

118) Where does Wash get hit when Tracey fires a gun on the bridge?

119) Why does Jayne say he didn't turn on Mal when Dobson offered him a deal?

120) What brigade was Mal a part of during the war?

121) What does Book give to Kaylee as part of the payment for his passage on Serenity?

122) Which crew member pushes Kaylee out of the way when an explosion occurs in the engine room?

123) Who refers to River as "a creature of extraordinary grace"?

124) Which crew members originally go out on top of Serenity to reprogram the disposal bin in "Trash?"

125) What does Mal tell Inara that he'll owe her as he prepares her shuttle for evacuation after the explosion in the engine room?

126) During dinner on Simon's first day aboard Serenity, what does Mal tell him that Jayne's job is on the ship?

127) What color is the dress Inara wears to the ball on Persephone?

128) What part of River's brain does Simon discover was "stripped" by the Alliance during his examination of her on Ariel?

129) Where does Mal inject Simon and River to wake them up when they are "dead" on Ariel: the neck or the arm?

130) What did Mal's mother do for a living?

131) Which character does Joss Whedon say acts as the narrator for the film *Serenity*?

132) During the flashback at the beginning of "Safe" when River is pretending to be fighting the Independents, what does River suggest to Simon that they might need to resort to after being cut off from their platoon by the Independents?

133) Who is hanging from Serenity's opening when the crew comes back to rescue River and Simon from their kidnappers in the episode "Safe"?

134) Who is the only primary character that does not appear in all 14 episodes of *Firefly*?

135) Which Serenity crew member stops playback of the recorded message on Miranda after the crew has finished watching it?

136) After finding Shepherd Book dying at Haven, who does Mal send to get the doctor?

MORENA BACCARIN
"INARA"

BIRTHDAY: JUNE 2, 1979
BORN: RIO DE JANEIRO, BRAZIL

Morena Baccarin is the daughter of Italian journalist Fernando Baccarin and Brazilian actress Vera Setta (who played a character named Morena in the 1976 comedy *O Vampiro de Copacabana*). Born in Brazil, Baccarin and her family moved to New York's Greenwich Village when her father took a job as an editor at Globo TV. In school, she says she was primarily interested in more academic subjects like math and science, but Baccarin admits that theater is in her blood. "My mom is an actress in Brazil, my uncle was an actor, my great uncle is a big theater director there," she notes, "So I grew up in the arts." In New York, Morena began following in her mother's footsteps by enrolling in the Fiorello H. LaGuardia High School of Music & Art and Performing Arts, where she studied acting. After graduating, she was accepted into the theater program at the Juilliard School.

After graduating from Juilliard, her first major acting role was as Natalie Portman's understudy in the Central Park production of Checkov's "The Seagull," which also included fellow cast members and Oscar winners Christopher Walken, Meryl Streep, and Phillip Seymour Hoffman. Her first screen role was in the independent film *Perfume* (2001), followed by a leading role in the film *Way Off Broadway* (2001), for which she won the Best Actress Award at the 2001 Wine Country Film Festival.

Baccarin's first television job was working on the Joss Whedon series *Firefly*. She originally had doubts about auditioning for the part of Inara, but she won over Whedon during her audition and quickly replaced Rebecca Gayheart, who had been originally cast in the part. Although the show was short-lived, it gave Baccarin exposure and a

fan base that would earn her many more opportunities to work on TV. She followed *Firefly*'s cancellation with appearances on television series such as *The O.C.*, *Kitchen Confidential*, and *How I Met Your Mother*, in addition to being cast in the series *Still Life* (which was cancelled before a single episode ever aired). In 2005 Baccarin returned to the role of Inara, this time for the feature film *Serenity*, which continued the story that had begun on *Firefly*.

Baccarin's popularity, especially among science fiction fans, helped her land her next television role, Adria, who made several recurring appearances as one of the show's main antagonists during the tenth season of *Stargate SG-1*. She was offered the role of Adria over the phone by the show's producers, who also happened to be fans of *Firefly*. She reprised the role a year later when the direct-to-DVD film *Stargate: The Ark of Truth* was produced. More recently, Baccarin was cast as Anna, the leader of the Visitors who come to Earth in a remake of the classic science fiction series *V*. During its two seasons on the air, Baccarin received two Saturn Award nominations for Best Supporting Actress on Television for her work. In the future, she says she would love to do more comedy (she cites *Modern Family* as one of her obsessions) as well as play Juliet in a production of Shakespeare's *Romeo and Juliet*.

Chapter Two
PLACES IN THE 'VERSE

137) When another ship finds Serenity drifting dead in space, where does that ship's captain say they just finished a salvage mission?

138) Where do Mal and Atherton Wing duel?

139) In "Bushwhacked," where did the transport ship that was attacked by Reavers originate from?

140) What is the name of the hospital that the crew robs on Ariel?

141) "Skunkworks" was the name of a building in Valencia, CA where episodes of *Buffy the Vampire Slayer* were filmed and was used during the production of *Firefly* as what location in the series?

142) The Lassiter is on display in what room before Mal and Saffron steal it?

143) What does Mal say are the only things that can be found on New Melbourne?

144) Where was Serenity originally headed before Saffron hijacked the ship in "Our Mrs. Reynolds"?

145) What feature of the ballroom on Persephone does Kaylee first take notice of when she and Mal arrive at the ball?

146) What is the town that Mal and Zoe arrive in after stealing Alliance goods off the train in "The Train Job"?

147) What planet is Mal referring to when he says, "I'm starting to find this whole planet very uninviting?"

148) Where does Mal meet Rance Burgess for the first time?

149) Where is Serenity headed before the events in "Out of Gas" take place?

150) Where is Serenity headed when Jubal Early sneaks on board?

151) What is the name of the town at the beginning of *Serenity* where the crew steals the security payroll and escapes from the Reavers?

152) In "The Message," where does Tracey say his home is?

153) On what moon is Canton located?

154) What kind of beach does Wash suggest they go to when Mal and Zoe return to the ambulance with the stolen medical supplies?

155) What was the destination of the transport ship that was attacked by Reavers in "Bushwhacked"?

156) Where is the crew originally headed after meeting with Badger and taking on passengers on Persephone?

157) What does Joss Whedon refer to as "the Jiffy-Pop mansion"?

158) On what planet was Simon a surgeon before rescuing River?

159) Where is the disposal bin with the stolen Lassiter in it reprogrammed to go?

160) What is the name of the process where uninhabitable planets are changed into planets with Earth-like gravity and atmosphere?

161) What does Jayne say the Heart of Gold looks like when he first sees it?

162) What part of the hospital are Simon, Jayne, and River in when Simon saves a patient's life in "Ariel"?

163) Saffron says she 'knows a guy' on what planet that will help them sell the Lassiter?

164) Where was Inara born?

165) True or False: Wash and Kaylee end up trapping themselves in the engine room when Rance Burgess's men ambush them on Serenity.

166) The owner of the Lassiter lives on what planet?

167) Where is the crew of Serenity headed after the payroll heist to meet Fanty and Mingo?

168) Whitefall is the fourth moon of what planet?

169) The hospital that Simon was a surgeon at before he rescued River from the Academy is located in what city?

170) On what planet did the Battle of Serenity Valley take place?

171) Where are Kalyee and Tracey when Serenity is being chased by Lieutenant Womack's ship?

172) What room number is the medical vault in the hospital on Ariel?

173) What is the sickness called that has affected the people of Paradiso?

174) At the end of "Shindig," where does Kaylee have her dress from the ball hanging: In the engine room or her bunk?

175) What color are the words "Kaylee's Room" written in on the door to her bunk?

176) What is covering the Heart of Gold that gives it its metallic appearance?

177) Where is Jayne when he says, "This place gives me an uncomfortableness"?

178) What room of the Alliance research facility is the Operative in when he meets Dr. Mathias?

179) In a DVD commentary, where does Nathan Fillion say was an excellent place on the *Firefly* set to take a nap?

180) True or False: The large puddles of mud in "Jaynestown" were natural.

181) Where does Serenity land when meeting Inara on Persephone?

182) Book is a Shepherd from what abbey?

183) What are the two primary central planets?

184) Where is the clinic that Tracey is supposed to be taking the smuggled organs to?

185) In what town do Mal and Zoe board the train before stealing the cargo for Niska?

186) The crew delivers the cattle they are smuggling to what planet?

187) Where is Book during the heist on Ariel?

188) What planet is Mal from?

189) In what city is the hospital that Simon wants to rob located?

190) Some of the rooms in the Heart of Gold brothel were wallpapered with what unusual material?

ADAM BALDWIN
"JAYNE"

BIRTHDAY: FEBRUARY 27, 1962
BORN: WINNETKA, IL

Adam Baldwin has made a career out of playing tough guys, whether military officers, federal agents, or characters who operate outside the law. Balwin got his break in acting when he was cast as the title character Ricky Linderman in the 1980 film *My Bodyguard*. Director Tony Bill discovered Baldwin while he was a student at New Trier Township High School in Winnetka, Illinois. He followed his big screen debut with a role in Robert Redford's Academy Award winning *Ordinary People* later that same year. After a number of supporting roles in TV movies and films, Baldwin was cast as the militaristic and savage Animal Mother in Stanley Kubrick's masterpiece *Full Metal Jacket* (1987). He continued being cast in military roles due to his size and height, including memorable parts in blockbuster films such as Major Mitchell in *Independence Day* (1996) and Captain Wilkins in *The Patriot* (2000).

In 2001, Baldwin's manager convinced him to audition for a new role being cast on the highly popular Fox series *The X-Files*. Series star David Duchovny wanted to reduce the number of episodes he would appear in during the show's eighth season, so a new partner for Agent Scully was being written into the show. As Baldwin remembers it, "I'd auditioned for the Robert Patrick role, but I guess I was wrong for it. Wrong age, wrong type, or just too tall for Gillian Anderson." But producers liked Baldwin, and created the recurring role of ex-Marine Knowle Rohrer for him. It was his role on *The X-Files* that caught the eye of writer/producer Joss Whedon, and soon thereafter Baldwin auditioned for Whedon's new science fiction series *Firefly*.

Baldwin's character on *Firefly* was Jayne Cobb, the ship's resident mercenary who surprisingly provided some of the show's funniest moments. Following the series' cancellation, Baldwin admits that acting jobs became scarce and worked for a time doing voice work for videogames and on the cartoon series *Jackie Chan Adventures*. After asking his former boss Whedon for a part, Baldwin was cast in the recurring role of Marcus Hamilton on *Angel* during the show's fifth and final season. Baldwin rejoined his former *Firefly* cast mates once more in 2005 to play Cobb in the feature film *Serenity*.

He returned to television and landed leading roles on Fox's *The Inside* and ABC's *Day Break*, both of which were cancelled after their initial thirteen episode runs. Then in 2007, Baldwin was cast as Major John Casey in the NBC series *Chuck*. Series co-creator Chris Fedak said that Baldwin was a perfect fit for the role, and the series aired on NBC for five seasons. During his work on *Chuck*, Baldwin continued to provide voices for animated films, including voicing the Man of Steel himself in *Superman: Doomsday*. He also played the character of "Disgruntled Bodyguard" in the 2008 comedy *Drillbit Taylor*, paying homage to the Linderman character that started his career almost thirty years before. "I had to convince them it would be okay to let me wear the *My Bodyguard* jacket, which I still have" he says, adding, "It still fits!"

Chapter Three
OTHER PEOPLE

191) What is the name of the leader of the settlement on Triumph where Saffron is living before stowing away on Serenity?

192) Who are the two people that shoot Tracey?

193) Where does the Lassiter's owner have an emergency signal located that he uses to call the police when he finds Mal and Saffron in his house?

194) Not including the mother, who else is in the room with Simon when he is delivering the baby in "Heart of Gold?"

195) When Mal is told during the Battle of Serenity Valley that they need a Lieutenant or higher to authorize air support, whose authorization does he use?

196) What article of clothing does Mal say his contact will be wearing at the Ball he and Kaylee attend on Persephone?

197) How does Mal eventually kill the survivor of the Reaver attack in "Bushwhacked"?

198) Who is Heinrich?

199) Who does Mal sell the cattle to?

200) The crew plans to pull off the payroll heist at the beginning of *Serenity* when everyone in town will be doing what?

201) In "Bushwhacked," what does the survivor of the Reaver attack do to himself that prevents him from being able to speak?

202) What is the name of the woman that assists Simon in treating people in the town he is taken to after being kidnapped?

203) What percentage do Fanty and Mingo say they want from the payroll heist when they sit down with Mal and Jayne?

204) Who are Mal and Wash on their way to sell the last of the stolen medical supplies to before being captured by Niska?

205) How did Mal originally meet Monty?

206) What is the full name of the man that owns the Lassiter?

207) What is the name of Serenity's mechanic before Kaylee was brought on board?

208) Although never said in the episode, what is the name of the party guest that chastises Banning Miller for being rude to Kaylee in "Shindig"?

209) According to the log, how many families were on board the ship that was attacked by Reavers in "Bushwhacked"?

210) What gift does Jayne's mother send him?

211) What is the name of the postmaster in "The Message"?

212) Who serves as Mal's second during the duel with Atherton Wing?

213) What position does Simon's mother suggest he might attain someday?

214) How does Jayne's mother address him in the letter she sends him?

215) Who is Mal's contact for the job in Canton?

216) What is the name of the sheriff in Paradiso?

217) What type of fruit is Badger peeling in his office while talking to Mal?

218) True or False: Badger's gang is made up of the same extras in "Serenity" and "Shindig."

219) What is the name of Magistrate Higgins' son?

220) Who refers to Badger as "a psychotic lowlife?"

221) During the Battle of Serenity Valley, what is the name of the soldier that Mal orders to provide cover fire while he and Zoe take over the anti-aircraft gun?

222) What is the name of the mute girl that River befriends when she and Simon are kidnapped?

223) According to the letter Jayne's mother sends him, what is Mattie sick with?

224) While investigating the derelict ship in "Bushwhacked," where do members of the crew find the bodies of the people killed by Reavers?

225) What is the name of the radio operator in Mal's platoon at the Battle of Serenity Valley?

226) Who does Mal run into in the hall after leaving Nandi's bedroom?

227) What is the name of the battle where Mal, Zoe, and Tracey are shown fighting together during the war?

228) What is the name of Rance Burgess's baby?

229) How does Mal say he can tell Fanty and Mingo apart?

230) What part of a woman's body is Badger inspecting as Mal, Jayne, and Zoe walk into his office in the episode "Serenity"?

231) Based on footage from his wedding, what religion is Mr. Universe?

232) Who is the dead man hanging in Niska's office when Mal gets details about the train job?

233) What is the name of the girl that is pregnant with Rance Burgess's baby?

234) What song is sung at Nandi's funeral?

235) According to Mal, what did Tracey do to Colonel Obrin during the war?

236) What does Dr. Mathias say is the main side-effect of his experiments on River?

237) Who is the warrior poet that both Shepherd Book and Niska discuss?

238) What does Tracey say he dreamed about while he was playing dead?

239) What is the name of the girl who betrays the Heart of Gold and tells Rance Burgess of the crew's involvement?

240) True or False: Monty picks up Mal and throws him to the ground to stop his fight with Saffron.

241) Who overrides the port controls and lifts the land-lock when Serenity is trying to leave Canton?

242) What does Mal tell Jayne about the women from the Heart of Gold that convinces Jayne to help them out?

243) Is Rance Burgess's newborn baby a boy or a girl?

244) Which crew member does Tracey ask Kaylee if she is romantically involved with?

245) What rank was Tracey during the war?

246) Who does Mal say has a "very fine hat"?

247) While examining Tracey after he wakes up, what medical emergency does Simon think Tracey is experiencing?

248) Who does Mal claim he came to Paradiso looking to get a job from?

249) What is the first name of Simon and River's father?

250) In his recorded message to Mal and Zoe, what does Tracey say was the one thing he couldn't survive?

251) What does Simon's father tell Simon he must do as repayment for getting him a dedicated source box?

252) What is the first name of Simon and River's mother?

253) What is the name of Mr. Universe's Lovebot?

254) In a flashback, who does Mal say has been trying to get Wash on his crew for months?

255) Who does Mal say is also looking into renting Inara's shuttle the first time he meets her?

256) What group of people does Dr. Mathias say have "personally observed" River at the Alliance research facility?

257) Who does Mal tell Zoe to contact about fencing the Lassiter once they've stolen it?

258) What does Jayne think is being smuggled in Tracey's body?

259) Who kills Nandi?

260) What is the name of the man Badger sends Mal to meet at the ball on Persephone?

261) What is the title of the client who comes to visit Inara aboard Serenity?

262) What does Durran Haymer refer to as "the only thing I truly treasure?"

263) Where does Mal suggest that the guard get shot during the payroll heist in *Serenity* because, "it'll bleed plenty and we avoid any necessary organs"?

264) Why does Mal's friend Monty look different since the last time they saw each other?

265) How many mudders does the foreman say he has working on his mud farm in Canton?

266) What does young River's teacher do during River's dream that causes her to start screaming in the Alliance research facility at the beginning of *Serenity*?

267) Who tells Kaylee at the ball on Persephone that her dress looks like it was bought from a store?

268) Who is Mal talking to when he says, "We are just too pretty for God to let us die"?

269) How much did it cost Simon's father to get Simon out of jail?

270) Who does Simon see walking on the street right after River disappears from the town store in "Safe?"

271) True or False: Mr. Universe's Lovebot appears with him in the hologram above his grave at the end of *Serenity*.

PHOTO COURTESY OF RAVEN UNDERWOOD.

NATHAN FILLION
"MAL"

BIRTHDAY: MARCH 21, 1971
BORN: EDMONTON, ALBERTA, CANADA

Long before becoming the lead in numerous network television series, Nathan Fillion envisioned himself following in his parents' line of work and becoming a teacher. But after some early success in Canada with various television and film roles, Fillion moved to New York in 1994 to break into mainstream acting. His first big role came when he was cast as Joey Buchanan on the soap opera *One Life to Live.* He continued on the show for three years, and in that time earn himself a Daytime Emmy nomination for Outstanding Young Actor in a Drama Series. Fillion's first big break in film came when he was cast in Steven Spielberg's World War II drama *Saving Private Ryan* (1998) as "the other Private Ryan," which was soon followed by his role as Alicia Silverstone's ex-boyfriend in *Blast from the Past* (1999). At the same time, Fillion was also making the leap into primetime network television during the second season of the ABC sitcom *Two Guys, a Girl and a Pizza Place* (which would lose the pizza place and be renamed *Two Guys and a Girl* by the start of the third season). After the show's cancellation at the end of the fourth season in 2001, Fillion would embark on the role that would help launch his career and transform him into a cult icon.

Fillion first auditioned for one of Joss Whedon's shows in 1996 when he read for the role of Angel on *Buffy the Vampire Slayer*. Fillion auditioned again for Whedon five years later, this time landing the role of Malcolm Reynolds, captain of the space ship Serenity in the Fox series *Firefly*. Despite positive reviews for his performance and favorable comparisons to Harrison Ford's portrayal of Han Solo, *Firefly* was cancelled by the end of 2002 after only 11 episodes aired. But during that run, Fillion had amassed a loyal cadre of fans (some lovingly referring to themselves as "Fillionaires"). Distraught over the cancellation, Joss Whedon gave Fillion a recurring part as the evil priest Caleb during the seventh season of *Buffy the Vampire Slayer.* But not one to sit idly by, Whedon continued looking for a new home for *Firefly,* and in 2005 Fillion and the rest of the cast reprised their roles in the feature film *Serenity.* Fillion would later comment, "There is nothing like a major motion picture to make you feel a little bit better about having your TV show cancelled."

He parlayed the popularity garnered from *Firefly* and *Serenity* into leading roles in smaller films like James Gunn's horror comedy *Slither* (2006) and the independent drama *Waitress* (2007), for which he received critical acclaim. He had also become an avid enthusiast of the XBox game *Halo,* and when the game's creators learned of his love of the game they cast him in several sequels, voicing the recurring character Gunnery Sergeant Buck.

Today, Fillion can be seen on the ABC crime drama *Castle,* where he plays the titular Richard Castle, a mystery writer who follows NYPD detective Kate Beckett (played by Stana Katic) and assists her in solving crimes. When not on set, Fillion is heavily involved with "Kids Need to Read," a charity he co-founded which serves to bring children's books to underfunded libraries.

Chapter Four
EPISODES

272) In what episode does River say, "I can kill you with my brain"?

273) In what episode do Wash and Zoe discuss having a baby?

274) In what episode does Inara kiss another woman?

275) In what episode does Jayne say, "I'll be in my bunk"?

276) In what episode does Inara tell Mal she is leaving Serenity?

277) In which two episodes of *Firefly* does Niska appear?

278) The crew celebrates Simon's birthday during what episode?

279) Which episode of *Firefly* does Joss Whedon say is like "a [19]30s William Powell comedy"?

280) In what episode is Mal referred to as "Captain Tightpants"?

281) When the episode "Safe" was too short just before it was scheduled to air, what scenes did Joss Whedon add at the last minute that he considers "two of the best scenes we ever did on the show"?

282) In which episode of *Firefly* are Serenity's crew members' true thoughts and feeling revealed through insights from River's perspective?

283) In what episode do we first hear River say, "Two by two, hands of blue"?

284) According to Alan Tudyk, he stole the 'Big Red Button' off the *Firefly* set during the filming of which episode?

285) Which episode begins with Mal sitting naked on a rock in the desert?

286) Which episode ends with Simon saying to River, "It's time to wake up"?

287) In what two episodes do the men with blue hands appear?

288) What was the last *Firefly* episode filmed?

289) What is the one episode in which the crew discusses Saffron but that she does not appear in?

290) In what episode is Inara's hair straightened for the first time?

291) In what episode is the phrase "Big damn heroes" used?

292) Which episode was written around a moment when Zoe would be forced to choose between saving Wash or saving Mal?

293) What episode begins with a majority of the crew playing a game in the cargo bay that involves throwing a ball through a hanging hoop?

294) Which episode does Joss Whedon claim largely "wrote itself" after he wrote the teaser introduction?

295) In what episode does Jayne's iconic hat appear?

296) In what episode does Jayne end up in the sick bay wearing a neck brace?

297) Which *Firefly* episode does Summer Glau say is her favorite?

298) What episode does Joss Whedon say he wrote because he "wanted to do an episode where River became a part of the group"?

299) What episode ends with Jayne saying, "Free soup"?

300) In what episode does Wash say, "Curse your sudden but inevitable betrayal!"?

301) Which episode does Alan Tudyk describe as "one of the more gun-battley" episodes?

302) In what episode does River slash Jayne with a knife?

303) In what episode does Mal say, "Jayne, your mouth is talkin'. You might wanna look to that"?

304) Which episode of *Firefly* does Joss Whedon say is his favorite?

305) What are the three episodes of *Firefly* that never aired during the show's initial run on Fox?

306) In what episode does Inara kiss Mal?

307) In what episode does Mal famously (and Nathan, spontaneously) pull Kaylee into a backwards hug while talking to members of the crew?

308) Who came up with "Shindig" as the title for an episode of *Firefly*?

309) In what episode does Mal say, "We've done the impossible, and that makes us mighty"?

310) Which episode of the series does Alan Tudyk refer to as "*The A-Team*" episode?

311) Which episode did Fox ask Joss Whedon to write as a replacement pilot?

312) In what episode does one of the main characters not appear?

313) Which episode does Tim Minear say depicts, "the extremes of savagery and bureaucracy"?

314) Which episode was conceived as "a way of reversing the Robin Hood myth"?

315) What episode of *Firefly* was being filmed when the cast and crew learned that the show had been cancelled?

316) Which episode of *Firefly* does Gina Torres say is her favorite?

317) Which episode of *Firefly* does Tim Minear say was "basically a submarine story"?

318) In what episode does Jayne talk about Vera, but she does not appear?

319) In what episode of *Firefly* does Joss Whedon appear as an extra?

RON GLASS
"BOOK"

BIRTHDAY: JULY 10, 1945
BORN: EVANSVILLE, IN

Ronald Earle Glass's interest in acting began in earnest after graduating from Saint Francis University in 1964 and enrolling in the University of Evansville in Evansville, Indiana. While there, he was encouraged to audition for a school play and became enamored with performing. After earning his Bachelor of Arts degree in Drama and Literature, he moved out to Hollywood to become a professional actor.

Glass' career as a screen actor got its start when he began making appearances on several popular television series during the 1970s, including roles on *Sanford & Son, Good Times*, and *Maude*. But his big break came when he was cast as Detective Ron Harris on the sitcom *Barney Miller*. The police comedy lasted for eight seasons, during which time Glass received an Emmy nomination for Outstanding Supporting Actor in a Comedy or Variety or Music Series. When the series went off the air in 1982, Glass quickly stepped into a new television role, this time playing Felix Unger in *The New Odd Couple*. The show was a reboot of the classic Neil Simon play *The Odd Couple*, which had already spawned a film version in 1968 (starring Jack Lemmon and Walter Matthau) and a television series that ran from 1970-1975. In this version, the titular characters were updated and portrayed by African American actors, including Glass and his co-star Demond Wilson. The show never managed to find an audience and was subsequently cancelled in 1983 after airing only one season.

After the cancellation of *The New Odd Couple*, Glass returned to making guest appearances on popular television shows throughout much of the 1980s, including roles on *The Twilight Zone, 227,* and

Family Matters. Although he was acting less and taking on fewer roles, Glass spent his free time exploring his spiritual side, and during this time became a practicing Buddhist. Speaking on the subject, Glass states, "It's the most profound and most correct world view that provides me with answers to all my questions." While he continued to make appearances on sitcoms, dramas, and kid's shows during this time, one genre that Glass purposefully avoided was science fiction. "I was a little afraid of science fiction," he says on the subject, continuing, "I never got into it and just skipped over it." That changed when an agent insisted he take a guest role on an episode of *Star Trek: Voyager* in 2000. Having whetted his appetite for the genre, Glass would enter science fiction history just two years later when he played Shepherd Book on Joss Weldon's series *Firefly*. After the show's cancellation, Glass briefly reprised the role in the film *Serenity*, and in 2010 a graphic novel was released finally unraveling the mystery of Book's past, answering questions that fans and Glass himself had been asking since the series began eight years before.

Today, Ron Glass continues to make guest appearances on television shows like *Shark, Dirty Sexy Money*, and *CSI: NY*. He's also recently made several high-profile appearances on the big screen, co-starring with Samuel L. Jackson in the 2008 film *Lakeview Terrace* and in the 2010 remake of *Death at a Funeral*. Besdies acting, Glass is involved with the Al Wooten Jr. Heritage Center, which provides afterschool programs and activities for children in the Los Angeles area.

Chapter Five
SHIPS AND VESSELS

320) What does the acronym ASREV stand for?

321) What is the class code of a Firefly transport?

322) What does Kaylee tell Simon is wrong with ships that have a Capissen 38 engine?

323) Serenity has V.T.O.L capabilities. What does V.T.O.L. stand for?

324) In what part of Serenity does Mal say it looks like "space monkeys" got loose?

325) In the episode "Bushwhacked," what part of the derelict ship does Mal send Jayne to in order to loot for supplies?

326) Before finding Serenity, what is the name of the ship that Book is originally offered passage on at the Eavesdown Docks?

327) What part of the ship flies off as she enters the atmosphere at the beginning of *Serenity*?

328) On what deck does Wash say that any valuables would most likely be stored during the crew's investigation of the derelict ship in "Bushwhacked"?

329) According to Zoe, what type of ship must have been used to take Mal and Wash off-planet after they are captured by Niska's men?

330) What piece of equipment does Mal bring with him to the Training House to prevent the Operative from getting a missile lock on Serenity?

331) What color is the ship that finds Serenity in "Out of Gas"?

332) After first finishing with the design for Serenity, what was the second ship that production designer Carey Meyer began work on for *Firefly*?

333) When the Alliance arrives during the crew's illegal salvage operation at the beginning of the episode "Serenity," Mal tells Wash to shut everything down except what?

334) Where does Saffron go to cry after Mal asks Shepherd Book about what he needs to do to divorce her?

335) What does Inara say that the 'funny smell' Jayne noticed in her shuttle is?

336) Who does Mal instruct to tie bodies to the nose of Serenity after finding the destruction at Haven?

337) What type of ship are the Reavers flying when Serenity passes them on the way to Whitefall in the episode "Serenity"?

338) How many Firefly class vessels does the Alliance commander say are "in the air" when Serenity's crew is detained in "Bushwhacked"?

339) What is the name of the Alliance vessel that stumbles upon the crew during the illegal salvage operation at the beginning of the episode "Serenity"?

340) What image is located on the front plate of the mule used throughout the series?

341) What part of Serenity does Kaylee say she needs to get to in order to bypass the booby trap set by Reavers in "Bushwhacked"?

342) What is the name of the Alliance cruiser that the crew takes Book to after he has been shot in the episode "Safe"?

343) What type of core does a Firefly have?

344) True or False: Inara's shuttle is docked on the starboard side of the ship.

345) What maneuver do Wash and Kaylee use to escape the Reavers on Whitefall?

346) How many breakers are there on the electromagnetic net that Saffron aims Serenity towards in "Our Mrs. Reynolds"?

347) What maneuver does Wash say he's going to attempt in order to rescue Mal, Zoe, Jayne, and River from the Reavers that are chasing them after the payroll heist in *Serenity*?

348) According to Kaylee, what is the only thing that was changed between the 80-04 and the 80-10?

349) True or False: During the maneuver to escape the Reavers on Whitefall, the starboard engine is the one that flips and reverses direction.

350) When the Operative suggests using the nav sat trajectory to track Serenity, how many total trajectories does an Alliance officer report finding?

351) Who is at the junkyard with Wash when he finds the ambulance?

352) The goods that Niska sends Mal to steal are located in which of the train's cars?

353) What part of Serenity does Mal tell Lieutenant Womack was damaged during one of Womack's warning shots?

354) At the end of "Bushwhacked," how many shots are fired from the Alliance cruiser to destroy the derelict ship that was attacked by Reavers?

355) What does Kaylee have to do in order to give the disposal bin with the stolen Lassiter in it new coordinates?

356) During their first meeting, how much does Inara tell Mal she will pay to rent one of Serenity's shuttles?

357) What does Wash do to the shuttle to prevent Mal and Zoe from leaving in "War Stories"?

358) Which crew member does Mal bring with him to tour Serenity after he buys her?

359) What word does Inara use to describe her shuttle the first time Mal shows it to her in a flashback?

360) In the episode "The Train Job," who drives the mule into one of Niska's henchmen during a fight in the cargo bay?

361) What color is the button that will call back both shuttles in "Out of Gas?"

362) Who is driving the mule after the payroll heist in *Serenity* when the Reavers are chasing them?

SUMMER GLAU
"RIVER"

BIRTHDAY: JULY 24, 1981
BORN: SAN ANTONIO, TX

The oldest of three sisters, Summer Lyn Glau's early life centered around dancing. At a very early age, Summer showed an innate aptitude for dance and earned a ballet scholarship with a local company in Texas. Her father Jim (a general contractor) and her mother Mari (a teacher) decided to home school Summer in order to accommodate her rigorous training schedule. For ten years, from third to twelfth grade, Glau would balance her life between her home schooling and her training. After breaking a toe and suffering from tendonitis in both feet, Glau's dreams of becoming a professional dancer came to an end. Although her injuries would prevent her from making a career of performing on the stage, they would not prevent her from putting her talents to use on television.

In 2002, at the age of 19, Glau moved to Los Angeles in order to pursue an acting career. One of her first auditions was for the show *Power Rangers Wild Force*, where she would use her extensive ballet training for the show's choreographed fight sequences. Despite losing the role (she was the second choice), Glau continued auditioning and went in for the role of a ballerina on the show *Angel*. After missing the dance portion of the audition, Glau completed her acting audition in front of series creator Joss Whedon himself. He quickly cast her in the role, and she auditioned for him again the following year on a new series he was developing called *Firefly*. After landing the series regular role of River Tam, Glau became one of the show's breakout stars, due in part to her graceful fight sequences and deadpan delivery of some of the show's funniest lines. Three years later, Glau reprised her role as River in the motion picture

PHOTO COURTESY OF RAVEN UNDERWOOD.

Serenity (2005). Glau acknowledges that she owes a great deal of her early success to Joss Whedon and his faith in her abilities. As she says, "Joss gave me my first guest-star on a TV show, he gave me my first series regular on a TV show, and he gave me my first lead in a film."

Following her sting of work with Whedon, Glau went on to appear in numerous guest roles on shows like *CSI: Crime Scene Investigation* and *The Unit*, and earned a recurring role on the USA series *The 4400*. But Glau's next big break came when she was cast as the lead in the Fox series *Terminator: The Sarah Connor Chronicles*. On the show, she played Cameron Phillips, a Terminator unit sent back to protect a teenage John Connor and his mother Sarah Connor. She once again utilized her background in dance to make the show's fight sequences balletic. The series would struggle to find an audience large enough to justify the show's budget, and it was cancelled after two seasons. Around the same time, Whedon once again came calling, this time looking to cast the character Bennett Halverson for a four-episode arc on his latest show, *Dollhouse*. More recently, Glau portrayed the mysterious Orwell on the NBC series *The Cape*.

Despite her hectic schedule, Glau says she still likes to dance and tries to find time to practice at least three times a week. As for her acting aspirations, she says she'd like to work on a romantic period film or a Western (she cites *3:10 to Yuma* as an example of a Western she really loved). However, after winning two Saturn Awards for her roles in *Serenity* and *Terminator: The Sarah Connor Chronicles*, it seems assured that her popularity within the science fiction genre will continue to grow and keep her busy with television and film projects for a long time.

Chapter Six
TIME

363) How much time takes place between the Battle of Serenity Valley and the illegal salvage operation seen at the beginning of the episode "Serenity"?

364) According to Mal, how long ago was the recording on Miranda made?

365) How long had it been since Durran Haymer had last seen Saffron?

366) Which character's birthday is February 15, 2484?

367) How long does Mal tell Wash it will take to complete the hospital robbery on Ariel?

368) At the beginning of the episode "Safe," the flashback to Simon and River as children takes place how many years before?

369) Wash once spent six weeks on a moon where the principle form of recreation was what?

370) What day are the bar patrons celebrating at the beginning of "The Train Job"?

371) In "The Train Job," how long does Inara tell Book she's been on Serenity?

372) How old is Magistrate Higgins's son when the magistrate brings him to Inara?

373) How old was River when she was sent off to the academy?

374) How long does Jubal Early say he has been tracking Simon and River?

375) How long had Jayne and his partner in Canton been working together before Jayne turned on him?

376) How often are Companions required to get a physical examination?

377) How many hours of oxygen does Kaylee guess they have left after the explosion in the engine room?

378) How does the crew learn it is Simon's birthday?

379) How many years in the future do the events of *Firefly/Serenity* take place?

380) How long was the herd of cattle on board Serenity?

381) Inara tells the sheriff of Paradiso that Mal is indentured to her for how much longer?

382) How many days does Niska say he wants to torture Mal for before he will let Mal die?

383) How many weeks did the Battle of Serenity Valley last?

384) How many years did the Unification War last?

385) Which of Serenity's crew members was born on July 2, 2497?

386) According to River, given adequate vacuuming systems how long does it take for the human body to be drained of blood?

387) On what date was *Serenity* released in theaters?

388) How old is River during the film *Serenity*?

389) How many months have Simon and River been on Serenity by the time the film takes place?

390) After Mal opens the container holding River, Simon states that she wasn't supposed to be revived for how much longer?

391) When is Mal's birthday?

392) What is Kaylee doing on Serenity the first time she meets Mal?

393) How old was River when she started correcting Simon's spelling?

394) After the Operative tells Mal, "you can't make me angry," Inara tells the Operative he should try spending how much time with Mal?

395) How long did it take for Nathan Fillion and Alan Tudyk to film the torture scenes in "War Stories"?

396) How long was Jayne's old partner in Canton kept in a box?

397) How long did it take Simon to finish his medical internship?

398) How old was Inara when she began her Companion training?

399) When is Inara's birthday?

400) In what month is Simon's birthday?

401) In what month did the first episode of *Firefly* air during its initial run on Fox?

402) Which two cast members were born on the same day, exactly three years apart?

403) Transportation of deceased human cargo through the Allied postal system is punishable with how many years on a penal moon?

SEAN MAHER
"SIMON"

BIRTHDAY: APRIL 16, 1975
BORN: PLEASANTVILLE, NY

Sean Maher first became interested in acting while performing in the play *Jesus Christ Superstar* at summer camp when he was a teenager. After camp he returned to Byram Hills High School and was cast in a production of *Bye Bye Birdie*, followed by another summer at camp, this time landing the role of Tony in *West Side Story*. He says of the experience, "I think that's probably the summer that changed my life. That's when I think it clicked." He continued performing in school plays and concerts, and even directed his senior musical. A talented singer, Maher originally thought his future would be in musicals, and not screen acting. After high school, he enrolled at New York University, where he earned a degree in drama in 1997.

Maher originally didn't intend on trying out for dramatic parts, assuming he had a better chance of landing roles in musicals due to his voice. But after auditioning in front of a casting director's assistant for a soap opera, she was so impressed with him that she encouraged him to get an agent. Soon after, Maher began the process of auditioning for television and he landed his first on-screen role as the lead on the series *Rayn Caufield: Year One*. Although he originally auditioned for a supporting role on the show, he eventually ended up reading again for the Caufield role and won the part. The series was cancelled after only seven episodes were filmed, an unfortunate fate that would plague Maher in several subsequent series. *Ryan Caufield* was followed by a recurring role as Adam Matthews of the popular Fox series *Party of Five* before once again being cast in a short-lived television series, this time on the Fox drama *The $treet*. In 2001, Maher landed the role of Brian Piccolo

PHOTO COURTESY OF RAVEN UNDERWOOD.

in the ABC television movie *Brian's Song*, a remake of the 1971 film starring James Caan and Billy Dee Williams.

Maher's breakout role came when he was cast as Dr. Simon Tam on the Fox series *Firefly*, which was again cancelled before given a chance by the network. Speaking about his succession of cancelled shows, Maher says, "I think the first time it happened, it was like a death." He says he often heard that his shows would be revived, and that by the time *Firefly* creator Joss Whedon promised to keep the show alive, Maher had his doubts. So when Universal announced that a film version of the show called *Serenity* would be made, Maher was floored. Speaking about *Firefly*'s ability to be resurrected when none of his previous shows were, he states, "I'm always so shocked at the *Firefly* phenomenon. It was the exact opposite of what I had been used to."

Since 2005, most of Maher's appearances have been guest starring roles on numerous television series like *The Mentalist, Human Target,* and *Warehouse 13*. He had a recurring role as Marcus during the second season of the ABC Family series *Make It or Break It* and was more recently cast in the NBC drama *The Playboy Club*, which was cancelled after only three episodes aired. Maher admits that while he loves working in TV and film, he misses living in New York and hopes to have the opportunity to do more work in the theater sometime soon.

Chapter Seven
BAD GUYS

404) How do Mal and the crew know that Patience is planning on double-crossing them?

405) During DVD commentary for "The Train Job," what fictional villain does Joss Whedon compare Niska to?

406) Of the two guards Jayne and Simon fight to escape custody on Ariel, how many did they kill?

407) Who was the leader of Jayne's old crew before he joined Serenity's crew?

408) Who does Lieutenant Womack threaten to light on fire?

409) What does the Operative tell Dr. Mathias his sin is?

410) What does Saffron promise not to tell anyone, if Mal promises not to tell anyone about her breaking down and crying?

411) Who kills Rance Burgess?

412) True or False: Zoe goes alone to bargain for Mal and Wash's release from Niska.

413) While trying to comfort Kaylee, what does Mal call the gunshot wound that she receives from Dobson?

414) What is Niska's henchman using to torture a prisoner at the beginning of "War Stories"?

415) Which eye did Jayne's old partner on Canton lose, his right or left?

416) Who is the second person to encounter Jubal Early once he is on board Serenity?

417) What name did Saffron go by when she was married to Mal's friend Monty?

418) What is the name of Jayne's old partner on Canton?

419) What does Mal do that Atherton Wing takes as a challenge for a duel?

420) What does Mal pantomime for Saffron to do when the owner of the Lassiter finds them?

421) Who is the first person to encounter Jubal Early once he is on board Serenity?

422) How many men has Atherton Wing killed with a sword?

423) What kind of dog did Jubal Early's neighbors have that he hurt and, presumably, killed?

424) True or False: Atherton Wing was a repeat client of Inara's.

425) Who does Joss Whedon say was the most difficult and the most rewarding villain to write on *Firefly*?

426) What name does Mal call Saffron that combines all of her known aliases?

427) What does Jubal Early think Simon says when he asks "Are you Alliance?"

428) In their first meeting, Joss Whedon told Nathan Fillion that all the bad guys on the show were going to wear what?

429) What does Inara offer Atherton Wing if he will let Mal live?

430) In "Bushwhacked," what does the Alliance commander refer to Serenity as, which Kaylee takes extreme offense to?

431) How many times does Mal stab Atherton Wing after Atherton is lying on the ground defeated?

432) What color is Jubal Early's suit?

433) What do the townspeople who kidnapped Simon and River accuse River of being?

434) What is the name of the bar patron who toasts to Unification Day at the beginning of "The Train Job"?

435) True or False: Jubal Early has an earring.

436) When the Operative is reviewing Mal's file, how many times does it say that Mal has been bound by law?

437) What does Jubal Early say he is after he tells Simon he's not a bounty hunter?

438) True or False: Mal introduces himself using his real name the first time he meets Rance Burgess.

439) What character does Joss Whedon describe as a James Bond henchman?

440) Which member of Jayne's old crew does Zoe say is the one that tracked them during a flashback in "Out of Gas"?

441) Who puts a knife to Rance Burgess's neck when he is trying to leave the Heart of Gold with his child?

442) What is the name of the man in Patience's gang who wears a top hat?

443) True or False: Mal first encounters Jubal Early in his bunk.

444) How much money does Mal say he wants before he'll tell Patience where the Alliance goods are buried during their meeting on Whitefall?

445) After his final battle with the Operative, which of Mal's eyes is bloody and bright red: his right or left?

446) What does Saffron tell her former husband happened to her after she was kidnapped from his house?

447) What is Niska's first name?

448) In what part of the body does Jubal Early shoot Simon?

449) Does Mal shoot Dobson in his left eye or his right eye?

450) Where does a guard bite Jayne during the escape from the hospital on Ariel?

451) True or False: In order to buy back Mal and Wash, Zoe offers to pay Niska four times as much money as Niska originally paid them for the train job.

452) Which Serenity crew member does Jayne's former partner on Canton find and beat up while looking for Jayne?

453) What is Dobson's first name?

454) What does Wash suggest that he could do to keep Lieutenant Womack occupied when Womack keeps contacting them in "The Message"?

455) What does Inara say that Atherton Wing has planned after he kills Mal at the duel?

456) What character does Joss Whedon describe as "The gentlest, kindest, most thoughtful person who ever killed a bunch of people that there was"?

457) What percentage of the people exposed to the Pax on Miranda turned into Reavers?

458) What body part of Dobson's does Jayne suggest he was planning on cutting off during his interrogation of Dobson?

459) How does Saffron knock out Wash when they are alone on the bridge?

460) At the beginning of "War Stories," why does Niska claim that his prisoner is being tortured?

461) What does Saffron offer to do for Mal after he finishes eating the supper she made for him?

462) What does Jubal Early say the bounty is on River?

463) How does Jubal Early knock Book unconscious?

464) What type of accent does Niska have?

465) When the crew is being held on Serenity by Badger and his men in the episode "Shindig," what is the first idea for a diversion that Jayne suggests?

466) Wash tells Saffron that he's married to a woman who can kill him with what part of her body?

467) What offer does Atherton Wing make to Inara?

468) Which of her aliases does Saffron admit to Mal is not her real name?

469) During his duel with Atherton Wing, is Mal stabbed on the right side of his body or the left?

470) True or False: Niska personally cuts off Mal's ear.

471) What does Durran Haymer say he thought happened to Saffron after the last time he saw her?

472) How many electrodes do Mal and Wash each have attached to them when Niska is torturing them?

473) Jubal Early once captured a midget that was wanted for what crime?

474) Not including snipers, how many men does Patience bring with her to the meeting with Mal and Zoe on Whitefall?

475) How does Saffron get snuck on board Serenity after being left by Monty?

476) How many darts hit Kaylee during the fight with the Reavers in Mr. Universe's complex?

477) What is the name of the Alliance commander in "Bushwhacked"?

478) Is Niska married?

479) What kind of bird does the Operative compare River to, which Mal notes used to represent a ship's good luck, "till some idiot killed it"?

480) What name did Saffron go by when she was married to Durran Haymer?

481) How does Saffron incapacitate the owner of the Lassiter when she and Mal are making their escape?

482) What was the name of Niska's lead henchman, whom Mal kicks into one of Serenity's engines?

483) What does Saffron pull out of her bag after Monty leaves her behind with Mal?

484) What nickname does Mal ask Atherton Wing if he can call him when they meet at the ball?

485) What does Saffron prepare for Mal when she makes him dinner aboard the ship?

486) How many people come aboard Serenity when Mal is attempting to deal for an engine part in "Out of Gas"?

487) Joss Whedon has said that Jubal Early deals with each crew member in a specific way, and that Early had to deal with which crew member using logic?

488) True or False: The device used by the men with blue hands causes the agent on Ariel to bleed from his fingernails, among other places.

489) What is the name of the gunner on Rance Burgess's hovercraft?

490) True or False: When Saffron asks Mal to give her a lift off the planet that Monty abandons her on, she suggests to Mal that he can stick her in a crate if he wants to.

491) When the Operative tells Dr. Mathias, "Secrets are not my concern," what does he tell Dr. Mathias *is* his concern?

492) What is the name of the agent that captures Simon, Jayne, and River in the hospital on Ariel?

493) How many men does River shoot without looking when the crew is rescuing Mal from Niska?

494) Where is Jayne shot during the fight with the Reavers in Mr. Universe's complex?

495) Where does the agent in charge on Ariel first begin bleeding when the men with blue hands kill him?

496) How much money does Saffron tell her "husband" (the owner of the Lassiter) that she promised Mal for bringing her home?

TIM MINEAR
"THE SHOWRUNNER"

BIRTHDAY: OCTOBER 29, 1963
BORN: NEW YORK, NY

Some might say that Tim Minear's television and film career began when he was a child. An avid fan of television (particularly *Star Trek*), Minear began making his first films in his backyard when he was only nine years old. As his passion for film grew, it eventually lead him to study film at California State University, Long Beach. He began his career by working on small budget features as an assistant director on films such as *Re-Animator* (1985) and *Dudes* (1987) and as a production assistant on the 1986 film *The Men's Club*. But Minear's most distinguished role in film is most likely the uncredited work he did as an assistant director on the Oliver Stone film *Platoon* (1986) when he was just 23 years old.

After working briefly as a script doctor on a number of films, Minear transitioned into the world of television and began writing for the Family Channel series *Zorro* from 1990-1992. His first break in network television came when he was hired as a writer on the ABC series *Lois & Clark: The New Adventures of Superman* during the show's fourth season. Minear spent one season on *Lois & Clark* before moving over to write for the fifth season of *The X-Files*. It was during this time that Minear was first exposed to a new series from Joss Whedon called *Buffy the Vampire Slayer*. At the time, Minear recalls thinking "I just don't get the show."

For Minear's next project he teamed up with fellow *X-Files* alum Howard Gordon as writer and producer on the ABC series *Strange World*. While working on *Strange World*, Minear was invited to meet with Joss Whedon to pitch episodes of *Buffy*. As Minear remembers it, Whedon loved his story ideas but had concerns about working together. Those concerns were apparently minimal, however, since

PHOTO COURTESY OF RAVEN UNDERWOOD.

the following year he was hired as a writer and producer on Whedon's spin-off series *Angel*, where he would eventually direct several episodes as well. After *Angel's* third season, Whedon asked Minear to serve as the showrunner on a new series he was developing called *Firefly*. Together Minear and Whedon wrote seven of *Firefly's* fourteen episodes and Minear directed two, including the final episode ever filmed, "The Message."

Following the cancellation of *Firefly*, Minear has become somewhat infamous for his track record of working on cancelled television projects. After *Firefly*, Minear worked as writer/producer on *Wonderfalls* (13 episodes), *The Inside* (13 episodes), *Drive* (7 episodes), *Terriers* (13 episodes), and most recently *The Chicago Code* (13 episodes). Despite his shows failing to meet network expectations, Minear doesn't harbor any bitterness. As he puts it, "my philosophy is always to try to make the first thirteen [episodes] its own unit of drama, so if that's what you end up with, just thirteen...it would be its own somewhat satisfying experience." In honor of his streak of terminated television series, Minear can be found using the handle "CancelledAgain" on Twitter.

Chapter Eight
WEAPONS, EQUIPMENT & OTHER SUCH SUNDRIES

497) What percent alcohol is there in mudder's milk?

498) Which Serenity crew member finds and starts playback of the recorded message on Miranda that explains what happened there?

499) How many men had come to kill Jayne when he first got Vera?

500) What is the name of the medicine that was in the crates taken during the train job?

501) What is Jayne referring to when he says, "Pretty cunning, don't you think?"?

502) What does the Chinese symbol beneath the floating hourglass in Inara's shuttle translate to?

503) What does Mal give himself an injection of after he is shot in "Out of Gas"?

504) What is the only non-dinosaur toy Wash has on his console?

505) True or False: One of the items on display in the room with the Lassiter is an arcade-style video game.

506) When River finds a gun lying on the cargo bay floor in "Objects in Space," who takes it away from her?

507) The Alliance flag is a visual combination of what two things?

508) In what order does Jayne tell one of the girls from the Heart of Gold that she should give him his guns during the battle with Rance Burgess?

509) Mal says that stampeding cattle that have no place to run are like what?

510) True or False: The gun that River picks up off the cargo bay floor in "Objects in Space" was unloaded.

511) Who gives the recording device with Tracey's message on it to Tracey's parents?

512) What does Mal say the cattle on his ship were fed three times a day?

513) What piece of medical equipment does Simon want to use during the hospital robbery in order to find out what's wrong with River?

514) What is a Griswald?

515) Who finds the recorder Tracey had in his hands when he is first brought on board Serenity?

516) What does Book use as a weapon during the fight with Rance Burgess and his men?

517) After retrieving his and Jayne's guns, what does Mal crawl to reach during the gunfight in "Safe?"

518) What kind of knife does Jayne use to pick up and eat apples with?

519) What does Mal wear on his necklace during the Battle of Serenity Valley?

520) What started the explosion in the engine room in "Out of Gas"?

521) What does Jayne have in his mouth while he is going through Simon's things after Simon and River have been kidnapped in "Safe"?

522) What kind of berries does River pick for Simon when they are kidnapped?

523) What does Inara compare fencing the Lassiter to?

524) According to Badger, invitations to the ball on Persephone are so hard to get that you couldn't buy one with "a diamond the size of" what?

525) What is unique about the hold-out weapon that Jayne tapes to himself at the beginning of the *Firefly* episode "Jaynestown"?

526) Zoe tells Book that during the war she knew a man who had a hole blown clean through his shoulder, and kept what in the hole?

527) When complaining to Mal about not visiting civilized planets where she can find work, what does Inara remind Mal that the cargo of their last smuggling job was?

528) How many horses are pulling the wagon with Mal and Jayne when they are disguised as husband and wife at the beginning of "Our Mrs. Reynolds"?

529) What does Mal grab out of a toolbox to use as a weapon against the Operative when they are fighting in Mr. Universe's complex?

530) As he is waiting for Dr. Mathias to die, what does the Operative tell Dr. Mathias' assistant he will need her to get him?

531) According to Saffron, how many Lassiters are still known to be in existence?

532) What does Kaylee say she "couldn't get a hold of" to make a better cake for Simon's birthday?

533) True or False: When the statue of Jayne is knocked over in Canton, the head of the statue cracks and falls off.

534) What is Simon's birthday cake mostly made of?

535) True or False: The weapon that Rance Burgess carries with him is illegal for private owners.

536) What is the name of the treat that River and Book have at the beginning of "The Message"?

537) True or False: Jayne gives River a gun to hold during their escape from the federal marshals on Ariel.

538) What does Jubal Early say he thinks is "very pretty"?

539) True or False: The Lassiter Mal and Saffron stole does not work anymore.

540) What animal do Kaylee and Inara claim to see wood carvings of in every supply store they go to?

541) What number is prominently displayed on the front of Jayne's t-shirt in the episodes "Safe," "Out of Gas," and "War Stories"?

542) What do Mal and Saffron pretend to be delivering when they go to steal the Lassiter?

543) What does Mal use to hit Jayne with and knock him out after the hospital robbery on Ariel?

544) When Lieutenant Womack informs Mal that he is in possession of stolen goods, what does Mal think he is referring to?

545) Where does Jayne tape the gun that he tries to sneak into Canton?

546) After walking in on Mal cleaning his guns in the dining area, what types of weapons does Inara say go to the far left side of the place settings?

547) What cargo does the crew smuggle off Persephone after Mal's duel with Atherton Wing?

548) How many bags of money does Zoe have with her when she arrives on Niska's space station to buy back Mal and Wash?

549) What does Jayne buy for the crew with his cut of the money from the hospital robbery on Ariel?

550) Whose gun does River find lying on the cargo bay floor?

551) Who knocks over the statue of Jayne in Canton?

552) What type of animal are some locals skinning when Serenity lands at the beginning of "Safe"?

553) What gift was Jayne given the night Mal was married to Saffron?

554) At the beginning of the episode "Jaynestown," what is Jayne looking for when he tears the infirmary apart?

555) What flavor does Kaylee try to make Simon's birthday cake?

556) What game are Mal and Jayne playing when Serenity lands on Ariel?

557) After Simon and River are kidnapped, what does Jayne find in Simon's belongings that makes him remark, "It's amazing we kept them this long"?

558) After Kaylee is shot by darts from the Reavers in Mr. Universe's complex, what does Simon say he needs from his medical bag to treat her?

559) What type of gun is Vera?

560) When asked what she thinks River will do next after the incident involving River finding a gun in "Objects in Space," Zoe replies she will, "Either blow us all up or _____"

561) What kind of knife does Jayne carry on his belt, which can be seen in numerous episodes?

562) What two types of dinosaurs is Wash playing with during the illegal salvage operation at the beginning of the episode "Serenity"?

563) What does River get Simon for his birthday?

564) What is a dulcimer?

565) What does Wash suggest the crew start smuggling that would be easier than cattle?

566) After Simon and River are kidnapped in "Safe," what does Jayne take out of Simon's suitcase and put in his pocket?

567) What is Jayne wearing around his neck while he is going through Simon's things after Simon and River have been kidnapped?

568) What does an indicator light on Rance Burgess's gun say when he is escaping the Heart of Gold and being chased by Mal?

569) What is the name of the card game that Book, Simon, and Jayne are playing in "Shindig"?

570) What is the name of the company that can be seen on the video phones on Ariel?

571) What color is the tie that Mal wears to the ball on Persephone?

572) What does Jayne decide to not give Simon and River while they are forced to wait in their cabin during Saffron's appearance in "Trash"?

573) What color are the flowers on the wreath that Saffron gives to Mal as part of the wedding ceremony?

574) What engine part does Kaylee tell Mal she'd like to get when Serenity lands at the Eavesdown Docks?

575) What color is the medical bag Simon uses in numerous episodes of *Firefly*?

576) What is the name of the decoy device used to distract the Alliance cruiser during the illegal salvage operation at the beginning of the episode "Serenity"?

577) What suggestion does Wash make about selling the stolen medicine from Ariel that would have made them even more money?

578) In a flashback to the war, what does Tracey eat while a battle goes on around him?

579) What part does Mal need in order to fix the ship after the explosion in the engine room?

580) What does Mal suggest that Wash do to boost the signal on the emergency beacon when Serenity is dead in space?

581) During a flashback in "Out of Gas," what engine part does Kaylee point out is bad that Serenity's original mechanic didn't notice?

582) What medication does Simon chastise another doctor for giving to a patient in the hospital on Ariel?

583) What is the Lassiter?

584) What does Simon give Zoe a shot of after she's injured by the blast from Serenity's engine room in "Out of Gas"?

585) What does Inara light in the Training House that the Operative mistakes for incense?

586) What is the full name of the Pax?

587) What does Simon tell Kaylee that the "alien" in the tank really is?

588) What does River jokingly say is wrong with the berries she picks for Simon when they are kidnapped?

589) Simon compares mudder's milk to a drink made by what ancient civilization?

590) What tool is River fascinated by in a supply store?

591) What does Kaylee consider buying Simon as a gift that he later calls "crap"?

592) How much cash did Jayne drop when escaping Canton?

593) What does Zoe use to knock out a doctor who gets involved during her and Mal's part in the hospital robbery on Ariel?

594) What game are Mal, Zoe, and Jayne playing at the beginning of "The Train Job"?

595) What does the sign at the base of Jayne's statue in Canton say?

596) What does it say on the sign the bartender points to when the holographic pool balls malfunction at the beginning of "Shindig?"

597) What does River take off Jayne's plate during the dinner scene at the end of "Safe"?

598) After being attacked by River with a knife, what does Jayne say that Simon owes him?

599) What number appears on the banknotes (paper money) used in *Firefly*?

600) What "problem" does River find in Book's bible that she calls an "early quantum state phenomenon?"

601) What color of highlighter is prominently seen on the pages of Book's bible when River is "fixing" it?

602) What does Simon ask his father to get him during the flashback at the beginning of "Safe"?

603) What does River think she is holding when she finds a gun on the cargo bay floor?

604) How was the Pax administered to the inhabitants of Miranda?

605) What product does River see an advertisement for that causes her to become violent in the Maidenhead bar?

606) What piece of equipment does Simon use to reattach Mal's ear?

607) Zoe states that she doesn't like a dress with "foofaraw," but if she were going to wear a dress it would need to have what?

JEWEL STAITE
"KAYLEE"

BIRTHDAY: JUNE 2, 1982
BORN: WHITE ROCK, BRITISH COLUMBIA, CANADA

Jewel Belair Staite has been a professional actress almost her entire life. She began modeling at age five, and by age six she had already moved on to acting. She was quickly recognized as a talented young actress in her native Canada, and by age twelve had appeared in three TV movies as well as guest starring on the Canadian children's show *The Odyssey*. She followed her success in Canada with a string of roles on American television, including appearances on *Are You Afraid of the Dark?* and *The X-Files*. In 1996, she was cast in her first leading role as Catalina on the Nickelodeon science fiction series *Space Cases*, which aired for two seasons from 1996-1997. During the tail end of *Space Case's* run on television, Staite had already moved on to her next television project, this time playing one of the leads on the Disney Channel series *Flash Forward*. Despite Staite being nominated for a Gemini Award for her work on the show, Disney decided to cancel the series after only one season. Over the next several years she would make recurring appearances on several TV shows, including *Honey I Shrunk the Kids: The TV Show* for the Disney Channel and on the Canadian mystery series *DaVinci's Inquest*. This was followed by another television leading role on the family drama *Higher Ground*, where she worked with fellow Canadian actor Hayden Christiansen.

Staite gained widespread recognition and global acclaim when she was cast in Joss Whedon's science fiction series *Firefly*. Despite being perfectly cast as Kaylee on the show, Staite said that she'd had a different role in mind when she auditioned. As she stated in an interview, "I actually wanted to audition for River, but I was told that Joss was pretty specific in wanting to see me read." After landing

PHOTO COURTESY OF RAVEN UNDERWOOD.

the role, she was famously told to gain twenty pounds in order to portray the bubbly mechanic and her character quickly became identified by her iconic rainbow parasol and antebellum pink dress. After *Firefly's* cancellation, Staite landed the role of Heidi Gotts for a four-episode arc on the Fox series *Wonderfalls*, where she was reunited with *Firefly* executive producer (and *Wonderfalls* executive producer) Tim Minear. In 2005, she returned to Joss Whedon's 'verse to bring Kaylee to life once again, this time in the motion picture *Serenity*.

Following her work on *Serenity*, Staite began making frequent appearances on the SyFy Channel's popular series *Stargate: Atlantis* as Dr. Jennifer Keller, the Chief of Medicine on Atlantis. Although her character was initially intended to appear in only a few episodes, Staite (and Keller) managed to become fan favorites on the show, earning her a role as series regular during the fifth and final season. Since then she has guest starred on television series like *Warehouse 13* and *Supernatural*, as well as appearing in several TV movies. In looking back at her career, it's easy to see why Staite has become one of the most popular and sought after actresses in science fiction. When asked why science fiction roles interest her so much, her response is honest and straightforward: "Because female characters in science fiction generally rock. They're strong, they're smart, and they're different. Plus, being worshipped by fanboys is kind of awesome."

Chapter Nine
FAMOUS LINES

608) What does Mal tell the people they should be looking at during the payroll heist at the beginning of *Serenity*?

609) What is Mal referring to that he says is, "a spectacle might warrant a moment's consideration"?

Match the Chinese used on *Firefly* to its English translation:

610) Dong ma	A) Bastard
611) Fei-oo	B) Butt
612) Gos se	C) Dog crap
613) Hwoon dahn	D) Garbage
614) Luh-suh	E) Hello
615) Mei-mei	F) Junk
616) Nee hao	G) Little sister
617) Pee-goo	H) Understand

618) What is Shepherd Book's response whenever someone calls him "grandpa"?

619) What are the first words Jubal Early says in "Objects in Space"?

620) Who is Wash speaking to when he says, "Were I unwed, I would take you in a manly fashion"?

621) Finish this quote from Mal: "We have a little problem with our entry sequence, so we may experience some slight turbulence and then _____."

622) To whom does Mal give the advice, "Someone ever tries to kill you, you try to kill them right back?"

623) Who is Mal speaking to when he says, "When I want a lot of medical jargon, I'll talk to a doctor"?

624) What does Mal say to the group of Alliance soldiers he initially encounters in a train car while beginning the train job?

625) Who tells Jayne, "That hat makes you look like an idiot"?

626) Complete this saying: "When you can't run, you crawl, and when you can't crawl, _____."

627) Complete Mal's line: "I'd like to be the king of all Londinium and _____"

628) Book suggests that if Mal takes advantage of Saffron, he will be sent to a "very special level of hell" reserved for child molesters and what other group of people?

629) Fill in the last line of this verse from "The Hero of Canton":

    Now, Jayne saw the mudders' backs breakin'
    He saw the mudder's laments
    And he saw the magistrate takin'

    _____.

630) Who is Mal talking to when he says, "you're my kind of stupid"?

631) What is the phrase Simon says that puts River to sleep in the Maidenhead bar?

632) What is Jayne's response when Mal says regarding the cattle, "You know, they walk just as easy if you lead 'em"?

633) After the hospital robbery on Ariel, who explains to Inara, "We killed Simon and River, stole a bunch of medicine, and now the Captain and Zoe are off springing the others that got snatched by the feds"?

634) Complete this Mal quote: "If you hand touches metal, I swear by my pretty floral bonnet _____."

635) What is the last thing Simon says to River just before she goes on the payroll heist at the beginning of the film *Serenity*?

636) What four words does Mal say when we first see him sitting on a rock naked in the desert?

637) Who says, "I always thought the name Serenity had a vaguely funereal sound to it"?

638) When asked about the Bible's policy on killing, Book replies that it is "somewhat fuzzier on the subject of _____"?

639) Who utters the immortal words, "Big damn heroes?"

640) Who refers to Book as a "Bible-thumper"?

641) What does Mal say when Inara asks him, "What did I say to you about barging into my shuttle"?

642) Book says, "A man can live on packaged food from here 'til Judgment Day if he's got enough" of what spice?

643) When Jayne is sent to pick up ammo in "The Message," he states that he "got a good discount on account of" what?

644) Complete this poem that Wash imagines he will give at Zoe's funeral: "Here lies my beloved Zoe, my autumn flower. Somewhat less attractive now that she's all _____"

645) Who says to Book, "Just keep walkin', preacher man"?

646) What is Mal referring to when he says to the Operative, "Of course, that ain't exactly Plan A"?

647) How does Wash define "interesting" at the beginning of *Serenity*?

648) Complete this line from Mal to Simon: "If I ever kill you, you'll be awake, you'll be facing me, and you'll be _____."

649) What is Mal referring to when he says, "This here is a recipe for unpleasantness"?

650) According to Zoe, what is the definition of a hero?

651) Who is Mal talking to when he says, "The next time you decide to stab me in the back have the guts to do it to my face"?

652) True or False: Inara refers to the girls working at the Heart of Gold as whores.

653) Finish this quote from Mal to Saffron: "I seen you without your clothes on before. Never thought I'd see you _____."

654) Which of Serenity's crew said, "A government is a body of people, usually notably ungoverned"?

655) When Kaylee is saying goodnight to Simon, she ends the conversation by saying, "Don't let the _____ bugs bite."

656) Finish this line from Jayne: "If wishes were horses,
_____."

657) What scene from the episode "Ariel" do Tim Minear and Joss Whedon refer to as "the Jesus Corleone speech"?

658) There is only one scene in the entire *Firefly* series where Book speaks Chinese. What scene is it?

659) When Wash and Zoe discuss having a baby, which of them says "I'm not sure now is not the best time to bring a tiny little helpless person into our lives."

660) Who is Book talking to when he says, "Yes, I'd forgotten. You're moonlighting as a master criminal now"?

661) Who does Mal refer to as a "prairie harpy"?

662) Which crew member, when seeing Jayne's statue for the first time, says, "Everywhere I go, his eyes keep following me"?

663) How does Saffron reply when Inara asks her who she is just before Saffron steals one of Serenity's shuttles?

664) What is the first thing River says after she slashes Jayne with a knife?

665) Who says the iconic line, "Can't stop the signal"?

666) Complete this line that Jayne worked so hard to memorize for the hospital robbery on Ariel: "We applied the _____ but were unable to get a neural reaction from either patient."

667) Who says, "Gee, I never been in trouble with the law before"?

668) What is the last word in the song "The Hero of Canton"?

669) Who says, "Everybody dies alone"?

670) What does Jayne ask Mal to do when Mal leaves Jayne in an open airlock after the hospital robbery on Ariel?

671) What does Kaylee refer to as "dead Bessy"?

672) Complete Mal's quote: "Well, they tell ya, never hit a man with a closed fist but it is, on occasion, _____."

673) What does River say after shooting Niska's henchmen?

674) Who is Mal speaking to when he says, "One of you is gonna fall and die and I'm not cleaning it up"?

675) What does Jayne say when River tells him Jayne is a girl's name?

676) During the episode "Objects in Space," who actually says the words, "Objects in space"?

677) Who calls Mal "Captain Tight-pants"?

678) What single line of dialogue is Joss Whedon referring to when he says, "there is no better statement about mankind's fate or, quite frankly, the fate of this show and how we felt while we were filming it, than what he just said"?

679) Who tells Simon, "You are such a boob"?

680) Who (or what) is Wash talking to when he says, "Do not fear me. Ours is a peaceful race and we must live in harmony."?

681) What two things does Mal pray to Buddha to bring him when he sneaks into the Companion training house to rescue Inara?

682) Finish this line from River: "She understands. She doesn't
_____."

683) Which crew member says, "Time for some thrilling heroics"?

684) What does Mal say when he regains consciousness after kissing Saffron?

685) After Tracey wakes up from being "dead," who says to Mal, "Your dead army buddy's on the bridge"?

686) Who is Mal talking to when he says, "You are going to be cleaning latrines with your face if you don't cut that out"?

687) Who does Jayne say used to tell him, "If you can't do something smart, do something right"?

688) According to Jayne, what is "the chain of command"?

689) When Inara asks Mal, "Will you wash it first?," what is she referring to?

690) What are the last words Jubal Early says when he is floating off in space at the end of "Objects in Space"?

691) Complete this Mal quote: "My days of not taking you seriously are certainly comin' to a _____."

692) Who is Mal speaking to when he says, "You'd best make peace with you dear and fluffy lord"?

693) What is the next line after Jayne pretends to read from Simon's journal, "Today we were kidnapped by hill folk, never to be seen again"?

694) After Saffron shows up on the ship and claims to be married to Mal, what does Mal say is the one thing he and Saffron have in common?

695) How does Mal respond when Fanty asks him (regarding River), "Do you know that girl?"

696) Who does Mal call a "genius mechanic"?

697) While talking to Kaylee in the film *Serenity*, Jayne lists five scenarios in which he'll kill a man. Name four of them.

698) Who is River talking to when she says, "I can kill you with my brain"?

GINA TORRES
"ZOE"

BIRTHDAY: APRIL 25, 1969
BORN: NEW YORK, NY

Gina Torres' career in the entertainment industry began not through a desire to act, but rather through her love of singing and dancing. Born the youngest of three children to Cuban parents, Torres says that being exposed to the Latino culture that permeated her neighborhood in the Bronx inspired her to pursue her passions. A gifted singer, she spent four years studying opera and jazz and performing on stage. She states, "I knew I could sing and then I got my chance to in a school play, that's when I got bitten." After graduating from the Fiorello H. LaGuardia High School of Music & Art and Performing Arts in New York (which was famously depicted in the 1980 film *Fame*), Torres decided not to pursue higher education, at least in part due to the cost. Instead, she began auditioning for theater jobs, and earned her first professional role on stage as Deena Jones in *Dreamgirls*. This was followed by numerous stage appearances in varied productions ranging from Shakespeare's *Julius Ceasar* to contemporary shows like *Blood Wedding*. Years later, Torres would reach the Broadway stage starring in *The Best Little Whorehouse Goes Public*, directed by theater legend Tommy Tune.

Torres began her screen acting career primarily through guest roles on popular dramas like *Law & Order* and *NYPD Blue* and in TV movies like 1994's *M.A.N.T.I.S.* She appeared on the soap opera *One Life to Live* from 1995-1996, but she became a recognizable face on the TV landscape when she made her first appearance as Nebula in 1997 on the popular syndicated program *Hercules: The Legendary Journeys*. Nebula would appear in numerous episodes over the course of the show's fourth and fifth seasons, and Torres' popularity on the show helped her land her first leading role on

Photo courtesy of Raven Underwood.

television as Helen 'Hel' Carter on the science fiction series *Cleopatra 2525*. After two seasons *Cleopatra 2525* was cancelled, and Torres followed it up with another science fiction series, this time as the first mate Zoe aboard Joss Whedon's Fox series *Firefly*. When the series was cancelled after only eleven episodes were aired, Whedon hired Torres to play the season four antagonist on his other series *Angel*. Around this time she also began doing more work on the big screen, most notably in the 2003 sequel films *The Matrix Reloaded* and *The Matrix Revolutions*, as well as reprising the role of Zoe in the feature film *Serenity* (2005).

Since then, Torres has made appearances on some of television's biggest series, including *CSI, 24, The Shield, Without a Trace, Alias, Bones, Boston Legal, Criminal Minds, Pushing Daisies, Eli Stone,* and *The Vampire Diaries*. Following her prodigious run of guest appearances, she has more recently been cast as Dr. Dorothy Rand in the short-lived ABC Family series *Huge* and as Jessica Pearson on the USA Network legal drama *Suits*. When asked about the multitude of shows she's appeared on in her career, Torres laments, "I never came out of the *Lost* jungle" and admits that she would have liked to have been among the survivors in the tail section of Oceanic Flight 815.

Chapter Ten
CAST & CREW

699) Morena Baccarin is a graduate of what prestigious performing arts school?

700) Which cast member is sometimes cited as being a "prop actor," and is usually holding a prop in many of his or her scenes?

Match the writer with the episode:
701) "Bushwhacked"   A) Cheryl Cain
702) "Shindig"   B) Ben Edlund
703) "Safe"   C) Jane Espenson
704) "Our Mrs. Reynolds"   D) Drew Z. Greenberg
705) "Jaynestown"   E) Brett Matthews
706) "Ariel"   F) Tim Minear
707) "War Stories"   G) Jose Molina
708) "Heart of Gold"   H) Joss Whedon

709) What was the last episode of *Firefly* that Greg Edmonson composed music for?

710) During their first meeting, which cast member told Joss Whedon, "I'm so not this guy"?

711) The 2007 and 2010 versions of the film *Death at a Funeral* each featured one *Firefly* cast member. Name both actors.

712) Who wrote the main title theme song for *Firefly*?

713) During a DVD commentary, which cast member refers to Inara as a "space hooker" and a "cosmic concubine"?

714) Hunter Ansley Wryn, the actress who played young River in *Serenity*, attended dance classes with which cast member's kids?

715) True or False: Ron Glass had long hair (like Shepherd Book) for five years before being cast in *Firefly*.

716) Who was the maid of honor at Jewel Staite's wedding?

717) *Firefly* writer Ben Edlund is well known for creating what comic book and live-action satirical superhero?

718) Name one of the two actors Adam Baldwin says were his inspirations for his portrayal of Jayne.

719) Costume designer Shawna Trpcic describes which character's clothing as "a very Banana Republic look"?

720) During the audition process for *Firefly*, who called Summer Glau to tell her she's gotten the part?

721) Who composed the music for *Firefly*?

722) Which fellow cast member does Nathan Fillion refer to as "Teddy Ruxpin good"?

Did the following production crew members work on *Firefly*, *Serenity*, or both?

723) Executive Producer Christopher Buchanan
724) Casting Director Anya Colloff
725) Composer Greg Edmonson
726) Editor Lisa Lassek
727) Producer Barry Mendel
728) Executive Producer Tim Minear
729) Visual Effects Supervisor Loni Peristere
730) Costume Designer Shawna Trpcic

731) What did Nathan Fillion write in a blog that he'd like fans to do if they ever see him on the street?

732) Which cast member is known for doing William Shatner impressions?

733) What does Joss Whedon say is "the most important book" he's ever read?

734) Which *Firefly* writer's first television writing job was an episode of *Firefly*?

735) What *Desperate Housewives* regular cast member had a guest role on *Firefly*?

736) Which *Firefly* writer invented the game Tall Card?

737) *Firefly's* director of photography David Boyd says he felt he got the job working on the series when he and Joss Whedon bonded while discussing what John Ford film?

738) In discussing his character's relationships on *Firefly*, what other character is Nathan Fillion referring to when he said, "whenever _____ says something to Malcolm Reynolds, Malcolm Reynolds listens"?

Match the character from *Serenity* with the actor who portrayed them:

739) Rafael Feldman
740) Yan Feldman
741) Terrence Hardy
742) Michael Hitchcock
743) Glenn Howerton
744) David Krumholz
745) Nectar Rose
746) Tamara Taylor

A) Dr. Mathias
B) Fanty
C) Lenore
D) Mingo
E) Mr. Universe
F) Reaver victim
G) River's teacher
H) Young boy at Haven

747) What book does Joss Whedon credit with inspiring him to create *Firefly*?

748) Which cast member appeared in two episodes of *Friends* as Ross Gellar's divorce lawyer?

749) Which cast member used the words, "Sex. Muscle. Humor. Thuggery." to describe their character?

750) What *High School Musical* star appeared in an episode of *Firefly*?

Match the *Firefly* guest star with their character:
751) Atherton Wing   A) Edward Atterton
752) Badger   B) Bonnie Bartlett
753) Dobson   C) Richard Brooks
754) Jubal Early   D) Melinda Clarke
755) Nandi   E) Michael Fairman
756) Niska   F) Christina Hendricks
757) Patience   G) Carlos Jacott
758) Saffron   H) Mark Sheppard
759) Tracey   I) Jonathan M. Woodward

760) Danny Nero, whose story was featured in the book *Firefly: Still Flying*, was the stand-in for what two cast members?

761) In addition to playing a madam in the episode "Heart of Gold," Melinda Clarke is also known for her recurring role as a dominatrix on what other popular television series?

762) Who said, "Nothing like a major motion picture to make you feel a little bit better about having your TV show cancelled"?

763) How many episodes of *Firefly* did Joss Whedon direct?

764) Who wrote the song "The Hero of Canton" for the episode "Jaynestown"?

765) What does costume designer Shawna Trpcic consider to be her "signature," which she incorporated into Badger's outfit in "Shindig"?

766) True or False: In real life, Ron Glass is an ordained minister.

767) Who performed the main title theme song for *Firefly*?

Match production crew member with their role on *Firefly*:
768) Production Designer   A) David Boyd
769) Visual Effects Supervisor B) Nick Brandon
770) Stunt Coordinator   C) Mark Cleary
771) Location Manager   D) David A. Koneff
772) Cinematographer   E) Jenny Lynn
773) Chinese Translator   F) Carey Meyer
774) Sound Effects Editor   G) Loni Peristere
775) Makeup Artist   H) Ron Pipes
776) Set Decorator   I) Peter M. Robarts

777) True or False: Jewel Staite's first audition for the role of Kaylee was in front of Joss Whedon himself.

778) Jewel Staite says that her favorite relationship to play on the show was between Kaylee and which character?

779) What other *Firefly* character does Sean Maher say he would have liked to play?

Match the director with the episode:
780) "Safe"   A) James Contner
781) "Our Mrs. Reynolds" B) Vondie Curtis Hall
782) "Jaynestown"   C) Vern Gillum
783) "Out of Gas"   D) Marita Grabiak
784) "Ariel"   E) Michael Grossman
785) "War Stories"   F) Allan Kroeker
786) "Trash"   G) Tim Minear
787) "The Message"   H) David Solomon
788) "Heart of Gold"   I) Thomas J. Wright

789) Kristian Kolodziej, who played the young boy in the episode "Jaynestown" that gives Jayne his knife back at the end, is related to what member of the production crew?

790) Which of the nine main *Firefly* cast members is the youngest?

791) According to costume designer Shawna Trpcic, a lot of Jayne's t-shirts said what in Chinese?

792) Of the nine main *Firefly* cast members, how many were not born in the United States?

793) How many people are 'hat-trick' actors who have appeared on *Buffy, Angel,* and *Firefly*?

794) Which two *Firefly* cast members attended the Fiorello H. LaGuardia High School of Music & Art and Performing Arts in New York City, which was the inspiration for the 1980 film *Fame*?

ALAN TUDYK
"WASH"

BIRTHDAY: MARCH 16, 1971
BORN: EL PASO, TX

Alan Wray Tudyk's journey to stardom began largely as a drama student while attending Lon Morris College in Jacksonville, Texas. He attended the two-year college from 1990-1991, during which time he received the Academic Excellence award for Drama and was voted "Most Likely to Succeed." After a few years off, Tudyk resumed his drama studies, this time enrolling in New York's prestigious Juilliard School in 1993. Although he would leave the conservatory in 1996 before earning a degree, his film career was on the precipice of taking off.

Tudyk landed his first film role in the independent film *35 Miles from Normal* (1997), followed by a small part in Robin William's *Patch Adams* (1998) the following year. But his first break in film came after shooting a small supporting character role in the Sandra Bullock film *28 Days* (2000). In the film, Tudyk played Gerhardt, a patient attending the same rehab facility as Bullock's character. Audience reaction was so positive to Tudyk's performance that the director asked him to shoot some additional scenes in order to wrap up Gerhardt's story arc just prior to the film's release. His improvisational skills and comedic timing led Tudyk to be cast in numerous supporting film roles for which he has become well known, including the character Wat, who serves as the squire to Heath Ledger's character in the 2001 film *A Knight's Tale* and the scene-stealing Steve the Pirate in 2004's *Dodgeball: A True Underdog Story.*

But for all his success on the big screen, Tudyk's real break came when he was cast as Wash, pilot of Serenity in the 2002 Fox series *Firefly.* Wash's witty banter and Tudyk real-life chemistry with his cast mates made the show loved by fans and made Tudyk one of the

PHOTO COURTESY OF RAVEN UNDERWOOD.

show's many breakout stars. After hearing of the show's untimely cancellation after a half-season, Tudyk famously removed the ship's 'big red button' from the set (used in the show to call the crew back together), and presented it to show creator Joss Whedon. Knowing that Whedon was looking to continue telling this story on another network or as a feature film, he included a note which contained a single line of dialogue from the series that summed up the cast's feelings: "When your miracle gets here, just hit this button." Although saddened by the cancellation, Tudyk endeavored to put a positive spin on things by throwing a "We Don't Work for Fox Anymore" party for the cast and crew. Tudyk and the rest of the cast were reunited in 2004 to begin filming the big screen follow-up to *Firefly*, *Serenity* (2005). Despite the fact that Tudyk's character does not make it through the end of the film, he remains optimistic that if a sequel is ever made, Wash will somehow be involved.

As with many Whedon alums, Tudyk was rehired by his former boss to play the cruel and mentally disturbed antagonist Alpha for several episodes of the Fox series *Dollhouse* (2009-2010). In addition, he continues to find work playing supporting roles in major Hollywood films like Judd Apatow's *Knocked Up* (2007), *3:10 to Yuma* (2007) with Russell Crowe and Christian Bale, and the most recent Transformers film, *Transformers: Dark of the Moon* (2011). But for all the fame he's garnered from his work on film and television, Tudyk has also strung together an impressive resume that includes numerous roles on Broadway and steady work as a voice actor in animated films like *Ice Age* (2002) and roles in the popular *Halo* video game franchise.

Chapter Eleven
BEHIND THE SCENES

795)   When River confronts Badger on the ship in "Shindig," what did the original draft of the script have her discussing with him?

796)   Whose idea was it to incorporate a sound montage over a black screen just before Mal wakes up in the infirmary in "Out of Gas"?

797)   Joss Whedon took the name Miranda from what Shakespeare play?

798)   What gesture did Alan Tudyk say he wanted to make to the alien in the glass container while filming "The Message," but Fox would not allow him to?

799)   Although the name is never said on the show, what does Tim Minear call the game that is being played at the beginning of "Bushwhacked"?

800)   What does Alan Tudyk say was his hardest scene in *Firefly*?

801)   Who does Joss Whedon credit with giving him the idea to make Inara the most cultured and educated member of Serenity's crew, rather than just a typical whore?

802)   What does Joss Whedon say were the two most important colors used in Inara's shuttle?

803) What does Alan Tudyk say he originally thought Wash did during the war?

804) Who was the character Two-Fry named after?

805) Who does Jewel Staite say was always nervous whenever they had to ride on the mule while filming episodes of *Firefly*?

806) What does Tim Minear say is the reason he wrote Zoe into a coma in the episode "Out of Gas"?

807) True or False: Wash's death in *Serenity* had been planned since Joss Whedon's first draft of the script.

808) How much weight does Jewel Staite say she was asked to gain for the part of Kaylee?

809) Of Serenity's nine crew members, which was the only one that Joss Whedon said remained the same from the show's initial premise through the actual filming of the series?

810) The original ending written for "Shindig" featured Kaylee in her ball gown dancing with who?

811) What element of *Firefly* does Joss Whedon say was intended to look "inefficient" and "like a city"?

812) True or False: While shooting the scene in "The Train Job" where Inara slaps Mal, Morena Baccarin had to wear a glove with padding because she was hitting Nathan Fillion so hard.

813) True or False: The prop bed in the infirmary was a working bed, that could raise and lower electronically.

814) After originally seeing his *Firefly* costume, Nathan Fillion says that he liked it because he looked like a "mean" version of what classic TV character?

815)   What does Joss Whedon say he wrote for *Firefly* before ever writing a single episode?

816)   Who does Joss Whedon say is the "Giles" of the *Firefly* universe?

817)   According to Nathan Fillion and Alan Tudyk, what had to be removed from Niska's torture room in "War Stories" for safety reasons during filming?

818)   What illustrator does Joss Whedon say served as the inspiration for putting Mal in a "pretty floral bonnet"?

819)   Chiwetel Ejiofor specifically asked Joss Whedon to film a scene of the Operative killing which character in the film *Serenity*?

820)   According to the DVD commentary for "War Stories," the colorful lamp on Niska's desk is from what company?

821)   Although it was cut from the episode, what was originally River's storyline that would have taken place during "Our Mrs. Reynolds?"

822)   According to episode writer Jane Espenson, the pool hall scene at the beginning of "Shindig" was originally written as what instead?

823)   Wash's Hawaiian shirt and flight suit look was inspired by a character from what classic science fiction film?

824)   In what episode does Alan Tudyk say they decided to abandon playing Wash as a calm pilot and incorporate more "Jerry Lewis" into his portrayal?

825)   Which cast member thought Joss Whedon was going to fire them during filming of the pilot episode "Serenity"?

826) What does Joss Whedon refer to as "The 10th Character" on *Firefly*?

827) Other than Alan Tudyk, who else was among the final two actors being considered for the role of Wash?

828) During the outtakes on the *Serenity* DVD, which cast member storms off the bridge and yells, "I'll be in my bunk!"?

829) What does costume designer Shawna Trpcic say was the biggest costume challenge in all of *Firefly*?

830) Whose idea was it for Mal to use the intercoms to speak to Jayne in the airlock at the end of "Ariel"?

831) Which cast member brought a didgeridoo to the set of *Firefly* and tried to get it worked into the show?

832) Why does Alan Tudyk say he hated the sweater he wore in the final scene of "The Message"?

833) What does Gina Torres say was the "toughest challenge" she encountered while filming *Firefly*?

834) What musical instrument did Mark Sheppard play in a band before making the switch to acting?

835) Which cast member does prop master Randy Eriksen say "ate like crazy" during the filming of the dinner table scene in the episode "Serenity"?

836) Rounded to the nearest hundred, how many extras does costume designer Shawna Trpcic guess were on set for the ballroom scene in "Shindig"?

837) Who would the cast routinely blame anytime someone messed up a line?

838) What set from the series was, as Joss Whedon described it, "basically a piece of every set that we'd ever built that we still had"?

839) According to Joss Whedon, one of the suggestions he initially got about Inara's shuttle was that it should look like what?

840) Who does writer Jose Molina credit with coming up with the idea to start the episode "Trash" with Nathan Fillion naked?

841) Writer Jane Espenson states that her legs were almost used in one scene to double for which actor's?

842) Which scene from *Firefly* does Joss Whedon say is like Tony and Maria (from *West Side Story*) seeing each other across a crowded room for the first time?

843) The dress that Inara wears to the ball in "Shindig" is actually whose wedding dress?

844) Whose idea was it for Wash to have a mustache in the flashback during "Out of Gas"?

845) What scene from the series does Joss Whedon describe as "one of those scenes you write and then you worry that maybe you're not as good a person as you hoped you were"?

846) While eventually expanding the cast to include the nine members of the ship's crew, how many main cast members did Joss Whedon originally envision *Firefly* having?

847) Whose *Firefly* costume does costume designer Shawna Trpcic say was partially inspired by other costumes she had seen in films like *X-Men* and *Daredevil*?

848) How many times did Joss Whedon shoot Inara's sponge bathing scene in the episode "Serenity"?

849) What two words did Tim Minear say to Joss Whedon that ultimately inspired Whedon to write the episode, "Objects in Space"?

850) True or False: The 'big red button' was brought back and incorporated into the bridge set during the filming of *Serenity*.

851) In the commentary for the *Firefly* episode "Serenity," Joss Whedon says that, "Apart from harness work, I don't think the actors hated me more for anything than _____."

852) Which cast member got married during the first four days of shooting on "Out of Gas"?

853) Instead of the Lassiter, writer Jose Molina says that he originally wanted Mal and Saffron to steal a copy of what iconic musical recording?

854) How many times does Joss Whedon say the Fox executives asked him to remove the word "humped" from episodes of *Firefly*?

855) What prop from *Firefly* did Ron Glass keep and eventually auction off for charity?

856) What prop did Adam Baldwin take from the set of "Jaynestown" on the last day of location filming, which had to be returned to the set later for an insert shot?

857) What character is Joss referring to when he said "_____ was designed just to be an asshole"?

858) What was the *Firefly* gag reel originally created for?

859) What does Joss Whedon say was "the most important scene in the pilot" because it "was the essence of the entire show"?

860) As an homage to *Star Wars*, Nathan Fillion and prop master Skip Crank inserted a miniature replica of what into the background of several episodes of *Firefly*?

861) True or False: Originally, Joss Whedon had envisioned *Firefly* as a show where guns were rarely drawn or used.

862) Production designer Carey Meyer claims that the book *City of Darkness – Life in Kowloon Walled City* by Ian Lambot and Greg Girard was an inspiration for what *Firefly* setting?

863) According to Morena Baccarin, during the filming of the ballroom scene in "Shindig," what did one of the extras tell her and Edward Atterton (the actor who played Atherton Wing) would happen to them?

864) What food item and brand of soda did Nathan Fillion have waiting for him to eat as soon as he finished filming the shirtless scene in *Serenity*?

865) In the commentary for the *Firefly* episode "Serenity," what does Nathan Fillion say is the one thing that will make him "cranky" on a set?

866) In an DVD commentary for the episode "Serenity," what does Nathan Fillion claim directly influenced Alan Tudyk's "frenetic panic" acting style when piloting the ship?

867) Which cast member broke River's cryo box prop during a rehearsal?

868) The term "futuristic CIA" has been used to describe what characters in the *Firefly* universe?

869) When it came to the fights during the filming of *Serenity*, what legendary actor did Nathan Fillion say he tried to emulate his performance after?

870) What was the first scene ever shot for *Firefly*?

871) True or False: Morena Baccarin wanted her hair straightened during filming the series.

872) According to Joss Whedon, which came first: the name *Firefly* or the design of the ship?

873) Whose idea was it originally to use whip pans and crash zooms to capture a more documentary feel to the space scenes in *Firefly*?

874) What does Morena Baccarin say was her most embarrassing scene to film during the series?

875) What does Alan Tudyk say was wrong with the "alien" prop from the opening scene in "The Message"?

876) Which cast member altered Book's prop bible by highlighting in it and tearing pages out in preparation for the scene where River is "fixing" it?

877) What does Joss Whedon say is the only flaw in how he designed Serenity (the ship)?

878) Tim Minear states that in writing "Bushwhacked," he was trying to "set up the [*Firefly*] universe by exploring the two extremes." What two extremes is he referring to?

879) What role was Joss Whedon originally going to play on the show?

880) Who does Alan Tudyk say was the person to go to when anyone wanted to know how to make scenes with guns "look cool"?

881) Which character from the film *Serenity* has Joss Whedon referred to as "the prince of exposition"?

882) The "Summer Blame Game" (where the cast would blame Summer Glau for mistakes made by anyone else on set) was started as a result of Summer missing her line in what episode?

883) What film does costume designer Shawna Trpcic say inspired many of the outfits in "Shindig," including Kaylee's dress and Mal's suit?

884) In the DVD commentary for the episode "Serenity," who does Joss Whedon say is the "Cordelia" of the show?

885) According to Joss Whedon, how long did he and Tim Minear have to write the script for the replacement pilot, "The Train Job"?

886) What prompted Joss Whedon to rewrite "The Train Job" so that Mal gives the medicine back at the end?

887) While working on *Firefly*, who does Morena Baccarin say taught her that, "you don't have to memorize anything until you get to the make-up room"?

888) Who was the Lassiter named after?

889) Who braided Ron Glass's hair for the filming of *Serenity*?

890) Whose idea was it to have River imitate Badger's accent in "Shindig"?

891) The hoop skirt that Kaylee is wearing under her ball gown in "Shindig" was borrowed from the Fox wardrobe department and was originally used in the making of what film?

892) What does Adam Baldwin say were "the most special times we were shooting" during the production of *Firefly*?

893) According to Morena Baccarin, what almost hit her "a couple times" while shooting the pool hall fight scene at the beginning of "Shindig"?

894) True or False: Wash's toy dinosaurs actually came from the home of prop master Randy Eriksen.

895) True or False: The basic idea for Jayne's hat was initially conceived when costume designer Shawna Trpcic noticed the production coordinator knitting a Christmas present for her mom.

896) How many hours of firearm training does Jewel Staite say she underwent to prepare for Kaylee's confrontation with Niska's crew in "War Stories"?

897) According to costume designer Shawna Trpcic, Zoe never takes off her necklace because it is representative of what?

898) Who helped Summer Glau work on the English accent she used in "Shindig"?

899) Who was originally cast as Inara?

900) Who was the executive at Universal who was largely responsible for getting the film *Serenity* made?

901) Prop master Randy Eriksen says that many of the blinking lights that can be seen in the engine room during early episodes of *Firefly* are actually what?

902) Jubal Early was the name of a real person that Joss Whedon used for the character in "Objects in Space." Who was Jubal Early in real life?

903) True or False: Joss Whedon considered killing off one of the crew in the first episode.

904) What scene does Nathan Fillion say he was shooting the first time he split his pants on the series?

905) True or False: Summer Glau wore a body suit while filming the scene of River emerging from the cryo box.

906) According to Joss Whedon, the phrase that Simon uses to put River to sleep in *Serenity* means what in Russian?

907) According to Tim Minear, the jail set from "The Train Job" was torn down and turned into what set for the next week's episode?

908) How many 'browncoats' were made for Mal to use on *Firefly*?

909) Who does Summer Glau credit with helping her get comfortable with the role of River by suggesting she "trust her instincts and her talent"?

910) What element of Mal's costume does costume designer Shawna Trpcic say was influenced by Han Solo?

911) "Rosie the Riveter" was an inspiration for the look of which crew member?

912) True or False: Nathan Fillion stated in the DVD commentary for "War Stories" that he fell in love with the *Firefly* theme song the first time he heard it.

913) Which character does Joss Whedon say had the skill to get people to talk about themselves and then would use it against them?

914) Of the nine main characters, which was cast last during the original casting process?

915) What scene from the episode "Serenity" did Joss Whedon show at Comic-Con before the series first aired?

916) In the DVD commentary for "Objects in Space," Joss Whedon states that, "nothing is more important in this episode than" what?

917) Who took the 'big red button' off the *Firefly* set and gave it to Joss Whedon?

JOSS WHEDON
"THE BOSS"

BIRTHDAY: JUNE 23, 1964
BORN: NEW YORK, NY

PART 1: IN THE BEGINNING...

Joseph Hill "Joss" Whedon comes from a long line of television writers, so it should have come as little surprise that he'd wind up making a name for himself in the same profession. Whedon's father Tom was a writer on many popular 1980s sitcoms like *Benson, Alice*, and *The Golden Girls*, and his grandfather John was a writer on classic series like *Leave It to Beaver, The Andy Griffith Show*, and *The Dick Van Dyke Show*. Whedon went to school at Riverdale Country School in New York, where his mother Lee taught history. From 1980-1982 he spent two years in England studying at Winchester College, a prestigious school for boys age 13-18, before returning to the United States to attend college. After graduating from Wesleyan University in 1987 with a degree in film studies, he moved to Los Angeles, where at the age of 25 he landed his first job in the television industry as a writer and story editor on the sitcom *Roseanne*. After writing there for one season, he became a writer and co-producer on the 1990-1991 series *Parenthood*, a television version of the popular 1989 Steve Martin film of the same name.

Following the cancellation of *Parenthood* after its first season, Whedon began focusing his writing efforts towards films. He had written the screenplay for the film *Buffy the Vampire Slayer* (1992) during his years as a TV writer, however when the film was eventually made the finished product drastically deviated from the story Whedon had written. Whedon was reportedly so infuriated by the changes that he walked off the set during filming and never returned. At this point, he began working in Hollywood as a script doctor, polishing and punching up film scripts that needed certain elements

Photo courtesy of Raven Underwood.

enhanced or reworked. Most famously he helped write the 1995 Pixar film *Toy Story*, which earned him an Academy Award nomination. Commenting on Whedon's role on the film, Pixar camera artist Craig Good remembers, "Joss took that [the original *Toy Story* script] and turned it into a cohesive script and, as you'd guess, came up with a lot of the great bits of dialogue." Although his work as a script doctor would largely be uncredited, he found himself working on some of the biggest films of the 1990s, revising the scripts for *Speed* (1994), *Waterworld* (1995), *Twister* (1996), and *X-Men* (2000). His work on film scripts also went on to include writing the science fiction sequel *Alien: Resurrection* (1997), as well as the animated features *Titan A.E.* (2000) and *Atlantis: The Lost Empire* (2001). During this time Whedon also made his first foray into the realm of music, writing the song "My Lullaby" for the direct-to-video film *The Lion King 2: Simba's Pride* (1998). Perhaps foreshadowing things to come, Whedon's song was so well received that it was nominated for Outstanding Individual Achievement for Music in an Animated Feature Production at the annual Annie Awards.

With a proven track record as a writer and an impressive body of work behind him, Whedon decided to embark on running his own show on the fledging WB network, where he would create one of the most iconic female characters of all time...

CONTINUED IN PART 2: THE WHEDONVERSE

Chapter Twelve
BEYOND THE 'VERSE

918) Which *Firefly/Serenity* cast member has been most closely involved with the Dyslexia Foundation, a charitable organization that works to help detect and prevent dyslexia and other reading difficulties?

919) What fan organization has been involved with numerous charity endeavors, including working with Adam Baldwin to sell screen-worn shirts and the Jayne hat for charity?

Match the Big Damn Hero to the superhero they have provided the voice for:

920) Morena Baccarin   A) Vigilante
921) Adam Baldwin   B) Superwoman
922) Nathan Fillion   C) Superman
923) Summer Glau   D) Supergirl
924) Gina Torres   E) Green Arrow
925) Alan Tudyk   F) Black Canary

926) What is the name of the fan organization (started in 2005) that found, purchased, and restored the ambulance from the episode "Ariel"?

927) Which female character does Adam Baldwin say would have been "the perfect woman for Jayne"?

928) When auctioned in 2008, how much money (rounded to the nearest hundred) did Jayne's Hat raise for charity?

929) In the one-shot comic *Serenity: Float Out*, three of Wash's old friends name their ship what in honor of Wash?

930) Name the four actors who have appeared in *Firefly* and/or *Serenity* who also make cameos in the fan film *Browncoats: Redemption*.

931) Who inadvertently started an Internet campaign to resurrect *Firefly* when they said in a February 2011 interview with *Entertainment Weekly* that, "If I got $300 million from the California lottery, the first thing I would do is buy the rights to *Firefly*, make it on my own, and distribute it on the Internet"?

932) According to the graphic novel *Serenity: The Shepherd's Tale*, what is Shepherd Book's real name?

933) In describing a scene that he never got to film for *Firefly*, who is Joss Whedon referring to when he says, "I had a whole thing worked out where _____ was going to go to a carnival and see [a Reaver] in a sideshow and then it was going to turn out to be a guy in a costume"?

934) What was the name of the uber-*Firefly* fan who created *South Park* style drawings of Serenity's crew and an online Browncoat Handbook before passing away in 2004?

935) Costume designer Shawna Trpcic say she would have incorporated her trademark pink flamingos into which main character's wardrobe, but never had the chance before *Firefly* was cancelled?

936) What two *Firefly* cast members appeared together in an episode of the SyFy series *Warehouse 13*?

937) When Nathan Fillion appeared on the cover of *Entertainment Weekly* in March 2011, what logo was on the t-shirt he was wearing?

938) Adam Baldwin has auctioned off many *Firefly* props including Jayne's shirt and the iconic Jayne hat to benefit what charity?

939) After a sold-out *Firefly* convention was cancelled the day before it was schedule to begin in December of 2006, California Browncoats organized a new celebration at the last minute that was called what?

940) How many of the nine *Firefly/Serenity* cast members appeared in episodes of *Dollhouse*?

941) Name the three *Firefly/Serenity* primary cast members that appeared in episodes of *Angel*?

942) What is the name of the astronaut (and Browncoat) who brought a set of *Firefly* DVDs to the International Space Station in June 2007?

943) How many of the nine *Firefly/Serenity* cast members appeared in episodes of *Buffy the Vampire Slayer*?

944) According to the graphic novel *Serenity: The Shepherd's Tale*, which of Book's body parts was replaced with robotics?

Match the character to the artist for the nine different covers of the comic "Serenity: Those Left Behind."

945) Mal

946) Jayne

947) Inara

948) Book

949) Kaylee

950) Zoe

951) Wash

952) Simon

953) River

A) Tim Bradstreet

B) John Cassaday

C) Jo Chen

D) Leinil Francis Yu

E) Bryan Hitch

F) J. G. Jones

G) Joshua Middleton

H) Sean Phillips

I) Joe Quesada

954) According to Joss Whedon, who do the Blue-Gloved Men work for?

955) What was the first fan organization to start a campaign to save *Firefly*, originally formed a couple of months before the show's cancellation?

956) Which *Firefly* writer edited the books *Finding Serenity* and *Serenity Found*?

957) What poem is Mal referencing when he discusses River with the Operative and says to Inara, "Yes, I've read a poem. Try not to faint"?

958) Other than the men with blue hands, what villain from *Firefly* makes a return in the comic book series *Serenity: Those Left Behind*?

959) The real Jubal Early fought in which war?

960) Which *Firefly/Serenity* cast member has been involved with Al Wooten Jr. Heritage Center in South Central Los Angeles, a charitable organization that helps underprivileged children?

961) What charity did Nathan Fillion help found in 2008 with author PJ Haarsma?

962) What character from *Firefly* did Joss Whedon suggest might make an appearance in a sequel to *Serenity* in an Internet posting shortly after the film's release?

963) Who wrote the introduction for the paperback graphic novel *Serenity: Better Days*?

964) In 2005, the ambulance from the episode "Ariel" was found in a scrap yard in what city?

965) Christina Hendrix has gone on to star in what critically acclaimed AMC series since her appearances on *Firefly*?

966) Which *Firefly* cast member has appeared with Adam Baldwin on the NBC show *Chuck*?

Match the cast member to their post-*Serenity* television appearance.

967) Morena Baccarin

968) Adam Baldwin
969) Nathan Fillion
970) Ron Glass

971) Summer Glau

972) Sean Maher
973) Jewel Staite
974) Gina Torres

975) Alan Tudyk

A) Conor Donovan (*Ghost Whisperer*)

B) Dr. Keller (*Stargate: Atlantis*)
C) Special Agent Kenton (*Bones*)
D) Him/herself (*The Big Bang Theory*)
E) District Attorney Ford (*Dirty Sexy Money*)
F) Dale Maddox (*V*)
G) Kevin Callis (*Lost*)
H) Chloe (*How I Met Your Mother*)
I) Bree (*The Vampire Diaries*)

976) Other than Wash, what character from *Serenity* makes an appearance in the Dark Horse one-shot comic "Float Out"?

977) If *Firefly* had continued, in what season did Joss Whedon see the events from the film (the crew finding out about Miranda and the Reavers) taking place?

978) What actor/comedian wrote the *Serenity* one-shot comic "Float Out"?

979) In which of the *Serenity* graphic novels published by Dark Horse does Badger make an appearance?

980) While many *Firefly* cast members were interviewed for the documentary *Done the Impossible*, name the two cast members who helped by hosting and narrating portions of the DVD.

981) What is the name of the *Firefly* fan-film/parody directed by Nathan Town that featured characters such as Cal, Chloe, Dry, Tome, and Winter?

982) Who wrote the novelization of *Serenity*?

983) What is the name of the completed *Firefly* script written by Cheryl Cain that was never filmed due to the series being cancelled?

984) One *Firefly* episode that was pitched but never scripted involved Inara training which fellow crew member to be a Companion in order to save the rest of the crew?

985) What NBC sitcom had an episode in which one of the main characters stated, "If one of us dies, we stage it to look like a suicide caused by the unjust cancellation of *Firefly*"?

986) What is the name of the company that produced trading cards for both *Firefly* and *Serenity*?

987) In an effort to prevent the cancellation of *Firefly* in 2002, fans raised money to place an ad in what entertainment trade magazine?

988) What is the name of the character that Nathan Fillion has voiced for the video game franchise *Halo*?

989) What CBS sitcoms features main characters who sign a roommate agreement which stipulates that Friday nights are reserved for watching *Firefly*?

990) What is the name of the *Firefly* fan film to which Joss Whedon gave his blessing and is considered an unofficial sequel to *Serenity*?

991) What is the name of the company that produces high quality and licensed collectibles and prop replicas from *Firefly* and *Serenity*?

992) Who wrote the introduction for the hardcover graphic novel *Serenity: Those Left Behind*?

993) Which *Firefly* and *Serenity* cast member contributed the essay "I. Malcolm" to the book *Serenity Found*?

994) How many of the nine primary cast members provided voices for the show *Justice League: Unlimited*?

995) Which *Firefly* cast member screen-tested for the role of Victor on *Dollhouse*?

996) What two *Firefly* cast members have starred on TV shows that were called *The Cape*?

JOSS WHEDON
"THE WHEDONVERSE"

The television series *Buffy the Vampire Slayer* (1997-2003) was a retooling of Joss Whedon's 1992 film of the same name, which had been completely rewritten during production in order to achieve a "lighter" tone and, in the end, drastically deviated from the original vision Whedon had for the story. The series was aired on the WB network, and remained one of the network's most popular shows for five seasons. In that time *Buffy* won an Emmy for Outstanding Makeup for a Series and Whedon was nominated for Outstanding Writing for a Drama Series, ironically for the season four episode "Hush" which found Buffy and her friends unable to speak. Following its fifth season, the series moved to the UPN network, which was willing to pay $2.3 million per episode for the show, as compared to the WB's $1.7 million. *Buffy's* sixth season included some memorable episodes, including Buffy's return from the dead, the death of Tara Maclay, and the musical episode "Once More With Feeling."

With the popularity of *Buffy* continually growing (along with the size of the cast), the spin-off series *Angel* was created after *Buffy's* third season. Set in Los Angeles, the series followed Buffy's vampire-with-a-soul ex-boyfriend Angel as he began working as a private detective. During the first episode, Angel discovers that fellow Sunnydale alum Cordelia Chase has moved to LA to pursue an acting career, and she is once again drawn into the world of the supernatural by helping Angel solve crimes.

While *Angel* was airing on the WB network, Whedon decided to move away from the supernatural and try his hand at science fiction. Set 500 years in the future, *Firefly* (2002) told the story of a future where the earth had become uninhabitable and new planets were transformed and colonized. The series followed the crew of the space ship Serenity as they tried to make a living through any means they could. Ultimately, only eleven episodes of the show were aired on the Fox network, but Whedon refused to accept that this was the end for his story. He vowed to find the show another home, and in 2005 the motion picture *Serenity* was released by Universal.

During the Writer's Strike of 2007, Whedon had the idea to experiment with creating Internet content that could be made outside the studio system and still be profitable. He called on many of his former cast and crew for help and spent six days shooting the website-crashing sensation *Dr. Horrible's Sing-Along Blog*. Although never aired on television, the three-part series earned Whedon his first Emmy for Outstanding Special Class – Short-Format Live-Action Entertainment Programs. In 2009, despite the heartbreaking cancellation of *Firefly* he'd experienced a few years prior, Whedon returned to work with Fox once again on the series *Dollhouse*. Starring Whedon's friend and former *Buffy* star Eliza Dushku, the show received lukewarm ratings but managed to stay on the air for two seasons. More recently, Whedon has been tasked with directing the superhero film *The Avengers*, due to be released in May 2012.

Whedon's work extends well beyond the screen, most notably including prolific runs writing for numerous comic book series including *The Astonishing X-Men* and *The Runaways*, not to mention several series based on his own creations. He recently contributed to the *Buffy: Season 8* comics, which are the canonical continuation of where the series left off. Whedon has also been an adamant supporter of women's rights, most notably through his support of the charitable organization Equality Now, which promotes and protects the rights of women around the globe.

Chapter Thirteen
DVD & TECHNICAL

Put the cast members' names in order that they appear in the opening credits of *Firefly*.

997) Morena Baccarin   A) First
998) Adam Baldwin   B) Second
999) Nathan Fillion   C) Third
1000) Ron Glass   D) Fourth
1001) Summer Glau   E) Fifth
1002) Sean Maher   F) Sixth
1003) Jewel Staite   G) Seventh
1004) Gina Torres   H) Eighth
1005) Alan Tudyk   I) Ninth

1006) What is the name of the visual effects studio that worked on *Firefly*?

1007) Jayne's gun Vera was actually a modified version of a weapon that was originally designed for what Robert DeNiro film?

1008) What three episodes of *Firefly* never aired during the show's original run in 2002?

1009) What kind of gun was used for the base of Mal's pistol?

1010) The main body of the Lassiter was made from what common household item?

1011) Zoe's 'Mare's Leg' pistol is actually a cut down version of what gun?

1012) During pre-production discussions regarding how a Firefly class ship would look and be laid out, which production crew member claims he "wanted Serenity's cargo bay to be detachable," like a shipping container that could be switched out for others?

1013) The Alliance sonic rifle featured in the *Firefly* episodes "Ariel" and "Trash" was based around a prop gun used in what Arnold Schwarzenegger film?

1014) As one of the special features on the *Firefly* DVDs, who is shown giving a brief tour of the set?

1015) In a deleted scene from the *Firefly* DVD set, who says to Book, "We want you to marry us"?

1016) True or False: There are actually three cows on set with Inara and Mal at the end of "Shindig."

1017) What recurring wardrobe element of River's did costume designer Shawna Trpcic decide to include to serve as a metaphor for her "hardcore inner character"?

1018) What does Joss Whedon say was the most difficult shot to film in the series?

1019) What was used to give the flashback scenes in "Out of Gas" their grainy and saturated look?

1020) According to editor Lisa Lassek, what is a "chone"?

1021) What sporting event often pre-empted *Firefly* during its initial run on Fox in 2002?

1022) Rounded to the nearest million, how much money did *Serenity* make in its worldwide theatrical run?

1023) The *Firefly* DVD box set contains deleted scenes for what three episodes?

1024) During the "*Firefly* Reunion" feature on the *Firefly* Blu-ray set, what does Alan Tudyk say he would like to see added to the Blu-ray release of *Firefly*?

1025) What is the only scene in the film *Serenity* that uses a miniature of Serenity instead of a computer-generated image?

1026) The crew's spacesuits used in *Firefly* were originally created for and used in what movie?

1027) The look of Jayne's pistol was influenced by a similar weapon that was made for what Jet Li film?

1028) Why did the production crew use a gas-gun rig to simulate shots from Vera instead of shotgun blanks in the episode "Our Mrs. Reynolds"?

1029) What 4 characters appear on the DVD cases in the original *Firefly* DVD box set?

1030) In the DVD commentary for "The Train Job," what movie does Joss Whedon say that he saw just before *Firefly* was first aired that incorporated zoom shots like those on the show, which made him upset?

1031) Zoe's pistol was originally created for and used on what TV show?

1032) What material was Mal's coat made of?

1033) A total of how many Alliance sonic rifle props were made for the entire filming of *Firefly*?

1034) Who sings the show's theme song as one of the special features on the *Firefly* DVD box set?

1035) Which episode of *Firefly* has commentary specifically recorded for the Blu-ray set?

1036) What is the name of the Los Angeles-based company that created Mal's gun holster?

1037) Which weapon from *Firefly* was made by Gibbons Ltd. and based on a Saiga 12 automatic shotgun?

1038) What 'Easter egg' can be found on the *Firefly* DVD box set?

1039) What memorable product from *The Simpsons* does Joss Whedon say the Fruity Oaty Bar commercial is similar to?

1040) Diamond Ranch High School in California served as the set during the filming of *Serenity* for what location in the film?

1041) Is the order of the nine principle cast members' names in the opening credits of *Firefly* the same order as the cast credits in the opening of *Serenity*?

1042) During a clip on the *Firefly* gag reel, shooting was stopped because a fly landed on whose nose?

1043) True or False: Composer Greg Edmonson wrote specific themes for several characters on *Firefly*.

1044) What Steven Soderbergh film does Joss Whedon say stylistically influenced the way *Firefly* was shot?

1045) What movie did some of the mudders' costumes in "Jaynestown" come from?

1046) What is the name of the Los Angeles prop shop that created Mal's pistol?

1047) Which character's primary gun was modeled around a Civil War era Le Mat Cavalry piece?

1048) In what year was the Collector's Edition DVD of *Serenity* released?

1049) What 'Easter egg' was included on the original DVD release of *Serenity*?

1050) *Firefly* won an Emmy in what category?

Answers

Key:

FOC 1 = *Firefly: The Official Companion Volume 1*
FOC 2 = *Firefly: The Official Companion Volume 2*
FOC 3 = *Firefly: Still Flying*
SOC = *Serenity: The Official Visual Companion*

Chapter 1

1) Sergeant ("Serenity," 20:49)
2) Kaylee ("Trash," 19:17)
3) Zero ("Objects in Space" DVD commentary, 15:57)
4) The right shoulder ("The Train Job," 36:57)
5) Fry cook ("War Stories," 15:21)
6) He will get very choked up (there could be tears) (*Serenity*, 16:02)
7) "My leg" ("Out of Gas," 12:02)
8) Three (DVD feature "10th Character," 3:28)
9) Kaylee (*Serenity*, 1:31:26)
10) Sake ("Objects in Space," 1:13)
11) Ten percent ("Serenity," 23:50)
12) Wash ("Safe," 17:31)
13) Zoe ("Objects in Space," 41:13)
14) 6,000 miles ("War Stories," 33:34)
15) She swallowed a bug (*Serenity*, 24:19)
16) Derrial (*Serenity*, 1:47:41)
17) Sponge bathing ("Serenity," 34:48)
18) Security payroll (*Serenity*, 16:35)
19) Captain Harbatkin ("Safe," 26:58)
20) Simon (*Serenity*, 24:25)
21) Mal punches him ("Bushwhacked," 17:21)
22) Jayne (*Serenity*, 20:04)
23) Mr. and Mrs. Raymond ("The Train Job," 28:43)
24) Eavesdropping ("Heart of Gold," 5:40)

25) Dishes and garbage ("Shindig," 15:52)
26) Jacks ("Objects in Space," 42:25)
27) Wash ("Out of Gas," 41:07)
28) Mal (FOC 2, p. 67)
29) Alleyne (*Serenity*, Alliance Database, Blu-ray Special Features)
30) Practicing for her dance recital ("Safe," 0:44)
31) Keelhaul them ("Ariel," 39:28)
32) Simon ("The Message," 2:38)
33) Wash (*Serenity*, 39:16)
34) Serra ("Shindig," 11:14)
35) Dancing ("Safe," 13:45)
36) River took Kaylee's apple ("War Stories," 4:51)
37) Kaywinnit Lee Frye ("Shindig," 13:35)
38) Reattached the patient's leg ("Jaynestown," 19:34)
39) To renew her Companion license ("Ariel," 1:46)
40) Dinosaurs ("Safe," 1:03)
41) "It's complicated" ("Ariel," 4:30)
42) He ordered her not to marry Wash ("War Stories," 20:54)
43) A statue of Hippocrates ("Objects in Space," 0:40)
44) The good-night kiss ("Our Mrs. Reynolds," 31:15)
45) Christmas ("Ariel," 27:36)
46) Russian nesting dolls ("Ariel," 41:22)
47) The chest ("Safe," 15:45)
48) Psychotic ("Serenity," 1:01:33)
49) Because they (Mal and Inara) didn't fight (*Serenity*, 49:50)
50) Kaylee ("Serenity" DVD commentary, 13:45)
51) She might see trouble before its coming (*Serenity*, 13:12)
52) House Madrassa ("Heart of Gold," 19:18)
53) Inara ("Safe," 22:30)
54) Jayne ("Bushwhacked," 15:46)
55) His toothpaste ("Serenity," 37:02)
56) True ("Bushwhacked," 12:19)
57) Wash, Zoe, Kaylee, and Jayne (*Serenity*, 48:38)
58) Rips the labels off canned foods ("Shindig," 16:30)
59) Wash ("Bushwhacked," 28:37)
60) Respectability ("Out of Gas," 27:57)
61) Complete autonomy ("Out of Gas," 26:47)

62)   Watch ("Shindig," 40:39)
63)   Mal punches Simon ("Serenity," 50:09)
64)   On his arm ("Ariel," 22:20)
65)   Jayne and Wash (*Serenity*, 1:09:39)
66)   Zoe and Kaylee (*Serenity*, 1:48:10)
67)   She lays on top of it ("The Message," 19:16)
68)   False. She supported unification ("Out of Gas," 28:38)
69)   Seven percent ("Out of Gas," 36:13)
70)   It spooks the cattle ("Safe," 3:03)
71)   Three ("Serenity," 45:00)
72)   Zoe (FOC 2, p. 67)
73)   Shepherd Book ("The Message," 12:02)
74)   Twelve bits ("The Message," 0:58)
75)   Lifting weights ("War Stories," 16:39)
76)   His right leg (*Serenity*, 22:23)
77)   Inara ("Trash," 37:27)
78)   Zoe ("Trash," 28:25)
79)   They will all freeze to death ("Out of Gas," 16:36)
80)   Three (Reaver victim 20:54, Reaver on Serenity (with Jayne and Zoe) 24:30, and Alliance ship survivor, 1:10:27)
81)   Jayne (FOC 2, p. 67)
82)   Her legs ("Bushwhacked," 32:09)
83)   His left ("War Stories," 27:18)
84)   She cuts his throat ("The Message," 8:02)
85)   Zoe ("Out of Gas," 8:18)
86)   Sharpening a knife ("Ariel," 2:17)
87)   She's using less oxygen ("Out of Gas," 14:58)
88)   Mal (*Serenity*, 1:05:31)
89)   Wash (FOC 2, p. 67)
90)   He has a mustache ("Out of Gas," 11:24)
91)   His right leg ("The Train Job," 24:10)
92)   He shot a man in the neck from 500 yards with a bent scope ("Objects in Space," 2:44)
93)   Simon ("Our Mrs. Reynolds," 7:39)
94)   Forty ("Our Mrs. Reynolds," 18:32)
95)   He believes Inara and Saffron kissed ("Our Mrs. Reynolds," 42:52)
96)   Daddy ("Safe," 31:34)

97) The Alliance "meddles" (*Serenity*, 1:44)

98) Hoban Washburne (*Serenity*, 1:47:44)

99) A trained ape ("Jaynestown," 1:02)

100) Mal and Simon ("Serenity," 41:00)

101) Inara ("Heart of Gold," 18:53)

102) Book, Kaylee, and Jayne ("Out of Gas," 24:34)

103) Suffocation ("Out of Gas," 15:30)

104) Kaylee ("The Train Job," 24:16)

105) Jubal Early ("Objects in Space," 25:52)

106) Lord Fauntleroy ("Serenity," 38:17)

107) His right hip ("Trash," 41:32)

108) Give him a tattoo ("Ariel," 14:14)

109) True ("Objects in Space," 2:00)

110) He was in a blackout zone ("Safe," 34:37)

111) Come rescue him (*Serenity*, 50:15)

112) Jayne (*Serenity*, 44:41)

113) Zoe is called "lamby toes" by Wash ("War Stories," 7:30)

114) His left shoulder ("Ariel," 11:21)

115) Three (The Reaver victim 20:54, the Operative 53:42, and the Alliance ship survivor 1:10:27)

116) Lifting weights ("The Message," 18:16)

117) True ("Heart of Gold," 19:22)

118) On his temple/forehead ("The Message," 35:34)

119) The money wasn't good enough ("Serenity," 1:23:18)

120) 57th Brigade (*Serenity*, 36:38)

121) Strawberries ("Serenity," 31:21)

122) Zoe ("Out of Gas," 8:03)

123) Dr. Mathias (*Serenity*, 3:25)

124) Kaylee and Jayne ("Trash," 21:00)

125) Her security deposit ("Out of Gas," 25:55)

126) Public relations ("Serenity," 34:10)

127) Gold ("Shindig," 15:07)

128) Her amygdala ("Ariel," 24:01)

129) The arm ("Ariel," 15:57)

130) Owned a ranch/ran cattle ("Our Mrs. Reynolds," 18:15)

131) River (*Serenity* DVD commentary, 2:37)

132) Cannibalism ("Safe," 0:36)

133) Jayne ("Safe," 39:14)

134) Book does not appear in "Ariel" ("Ariel," 1:29)
135) Wash (*Serenity*, 1:20:03)
136) Jayne (*Serenity*, 1:05:32)

CHAPTER 2

137) Ita Moon ("Out of Gas," 33:39)
138) Cadrie Pond ("Shindig," 25:49)
139) Bernadette ("Bushwhacked," 26:45)
140) St. Lucy's ("Ariel," 7:32)
141) The hospital on Ariel (FOC 2, p. 69)
142) The parlor ("Trash," 19:01)
143) Fish and fish-related activities ("Objects in Space," 3:40)
144) Beaumonde ("Our Mrs. Reynolds," 1:38)
145) The chandelier ("Shindig," 14:40)
146) Paradiso ("The Train Job," 16:10)
147) Jiangyin ("Safe," 12:52)
148) At the theater ("Heart of Gold," 11:23)
149) Greenleaf ("Out of Gas," 5:21)
150) New Melbourne ("Objects in Space," 3:38)
151) Lilac (SOC, p. 60)
152) St. Albans ("The Message," 13:32)
153) Higgins' Moon ("Jaynestown," 1:10)
154) A naked beach ("Ariel," 26:53)
155) Newhall ("Bushwhacked," 26:48)
156) Boros ("Serenity," 12:58)
157) The Heart of Gold brothel (FOC 2, p. 169)
158) Osiris ("Serenity," 33:00)
159) Isis Canyon ("Trash," 20:12)
160) Terraforming (SOC p. 12)
161) A frozen dinner pack ("Heart of Gold," 7:44)
162) The recovery ward ("Ariel," 18:35)
163) Persephone ("Trash," 15:02)
164) Sihnon ("Serenity," 15:05)
165) False. Only Wash is trapped in the engine room ("Heart of Gold," 34:55)
166) Bellerophon ("Trash," 12:57)

167) Beaumonde (*Serenity*, 24:56)
168) Athens ("Serenity," 28:39)
169) Capital City ("Safe," 19:09)
170) Hera ("Bushwhacked," 35:55)
171) In Kaylee's bunk ("The Message," 29:01)
172) 1205 ("Ariel," 21:16)
173) Bowden's malady ("The Train Job," 29:35)
174) Her bunk ("Shindig," 41:21)
175) Yellow ("Shindig," 41:02)
176) Solar sheeting ("Heart of Gold," 7:45)
177) An Alliance cruiser ("Safe," 29:00)
178) The records room (*Serenity*, 5:22)
179) Inara's shuttle ("Our Mrs. Reynolds" Blu-ray commentary, 15:01)
180) False. They were created for the show (FOC 2, p. 16)
181) Eavesdown Docks ("Serenity," 16:33)
182) The Southdown Abbey ("Serenity," 23:04)
183) Sihnon and Londinium (SOC, p. 12)
184) On Ariel ("The Message," 26:22)
185) Hancock ("The Train Job," 16:09)
186) Jiangyin ("Safe," 6:09)
187) The Bathgate Abbey ("Ariel," 1:29)
188) Shadow ("Our Mrs. Reynolds," 18:15)
189) Ariel City ("Ariel," 6:30)
190) Newspapers (FOC 2, p. 160)

CHAPTER 3

191) Elder Gommen ("Our Mrs. Reynolds," 3:45)
192) Zoe and Mal ("The Message," 35:37 & 37:57)
193) On his ring ("Trash," 30:17)
194) Inara and River ("Heart of Gold," 33:35)
195) Lt. Baker ("Serenity," 1:02)
196) A red sash ("Shindig," 15:12)
197) Snaps his neck ("Bushwhacked," 42:22)
198) The security programmer on Bellerophon that Saffron ran off with ("Trash," 25:41)

199) The Grange brothers (Marcus and Nathaniel) ("Safe," 10:47)
200) Attending Sunday worship (*Serenity*, 15:38)
201) He splits his tongue down the middle ("Bushwhacked," 36:45)
202) Doralee ("Safe," 25:23)
203) Forty percent (*Serenity*, 32:55)
204) Bosch (or Bolles) ("War Stories," 12:42 or FOC 2, p. 90)
205) They fought in the war together ("Trash," 6:30)
206) Durran Haymer ("Trash," 12:15)
207) Bester ("Out of Gas," 18:45)
208) Murphy (FOC 1, p. 117)
209) Sixteen ("Bushwhacked," 11:35)
210) A knitted hat ("The Message," 5:09)
211) Amnon ("The Message," 3:48)
212) Warrick Harrow ("Shindig," 26:25)
213) Medical Elect ("Safe," 19:12)
214) "My dear boy" ("The Message," 4:45)
215) Kessler ("Jaynestown," 5:50)
216) Bourne (FOC 1, p. 66)
217) An apple ("Serenity," 19:57)
218) True (FOC 1, p. 110)
219) Fess Higgins ("Jaynestown," 18:16)
220) Warrick Harrow ("Shindig," 21:50)
221) Bendis ("Serenity," 1:16)
222) Ruby ("Safe," 28:01)
223) The Damplung ("The Message," 4:58)
224) Hanging from the ceiling ("Bushwhacked," 15:23)
225) Graydon (FOC 1, p. 14)
226) Inara ("Heart of Gold," 26:27)
227) The Battle of Du-Khang ("The Message," 7:02)
228) Jonah ("Heart of Gold," 37:52)
229) Fanty's prettier (*Serenity*, 32:16)
230) Her teeth ("Serenity," 19:05)
231) Jewish (*Serenity*, 40:45)
232) The nephew of Niska's wife ("The Train Job," 15:49)
233) Petaline ("Heart of Gold," 1:30)
234) "Amazing Grace" ("Heart of Gold," 38:29)

235) Cut off his moustache ("The Message," 19:59)

236) She's unstable (*Serenity*, 2:38)

237) Shan Yu ("War Stories," 0:03)

238) His family ("The Message," 24:12)

239) Chari ("Heart of Gold," 25:08)

240) False. He picks them both off the ground and holds them apart. ("Trash," 3:41)

241) Fess Higgins, the magistrate's son ("Jaynestown," 39:45)

242) They're whores ("Heart of Gold," 7:26)

243) A boy ("Heart of Gold," 35:10)

244) Wash ("The Message," 29:29)

245) Private ("The Message," 23:33)

246) Badger ("Serenity," 21:37)

247) A heart attack ("The Message," 25:00)

248) Joey Bloggs ("The Train Job," 29:13)

249) Gabriel (FOC 1, p. 126)

250) The real world ("The Message," 13:44)

251) Become a brilliant doctor ("Safe," 1:53)

252) Regan (FOC 1, p. 126)

253) Lenore (*Serenity*, 40:41)

254) Renshaw ("Out of Gas," 12:07)

255) A surveyor and his wife ("Out of Gas," 26:16)

256) "Key members of parliament" (*Serenity*, 3:08)

257) Brennert and Ellison ("Trash," 42:21)

258) Gold ("The Message," 22:35)

259) Rance Burgess ("Heart of Gold," 36:00)

260) Warrick Harrow ("Shindig," 9:13)

261) Counselor ("War Stories," 10:58)

262) Saffron ("Trash," 24:27)

263) The leg (*Serenity*, 19:57)

264) Monty shaved off his beard ("Trash," 1:30)

265) Over two thousand ("Jaynestown,"4:40)

266) Her teacher stabs River in the forehead with a stylus (*Serenity*, 2:08)

267) Banning Miller ("Shindig," 20:14)

268) Bendis ("Serenity," 3:56)

269) 2,000 credits ("Safe," 34:20)

270) Local officers ("Safe," 11:56)
271) True (*Serenity*, 1:47:43)

CHAPTER 4

272) "Trash" ("Trash," 41:05)
273) "Heart of Gold" ("Heart of Gold," 16:43)
274) "War Stories" ("War Stories," 14:45)
275) "War Stories" ("War Stories," 11:34)
276) "Heart of Gold" ("Heart of Gold," 41:24)
277) "The Train Job" and "War Stories" ("The Train Job," 13:50 & "War Stories," 2:20)
278) "Out of Gas" ("Out of Gas," 6:47)
279) "Our Mrs. Reynolds" ("The Train Job" DVD commentary, 19:49)
280) "Shindig" ("Shindig," 14:58)
281) Jayne going through Simon's things and welcoming him back on board (FOC 1, p. 126)
282) "Objects in Space" (FOC 2, p. 187)
283) "The Train Job" ("The Train Job," 27:28)
284) "The Message" ("The Message" DVD commentary, 32:35)
285) "Trash" ("Trash," 0:06)
286) "Ariel" ("Ariel," 41:53)
287) "The Train Job" and "Ariel" ("The Train Job," 41:38 & "Ariel," 32:45)
288) "The Message" (FOC 2, p. 138)
289) "The Message" ("The Message," 21:13)
290) "The Message" ("The Message" DVD commentary, 3:21)
291) "Safe" ("Safe," 39:31)
292) "War Stories" (FOC 2, p. 86)
293) "Bushwhacked" ("Bushwhacked," 0:05)
294) "Our Mrs. Reynolds" (FOC 1, p. 156)
295) "The Message" ("The Message," 5:09)
296) "Trash" ("Trash," 38:36)
297) "Objects in Space" (FOC 2, p. 205)
298) "Objects in Space" ("Objects in Space" DVD commentary, 2:53)

299) "War Stories" ("War Stories," 42:03)
300) "Serenity" ("Serenity," 6:37)
301) "War Stories" ("War Stories" DVD commentary, 31:59)
302) "Ariel" ("Ariel," 2:17)
303) "Serenity" ("Serenity," 24:19)
304) "Out of Gas" (FOC 2, p. 47)
305) "Trash," "The Message," and "Heart of Gold" (*Firefly* DVD box set)
306) "Our Mrs. Reynolds" ("Our Mrs. Reynolds," 31:17)
307) "Ariel" ("Ariel," 37:02)
308) Jane Espenson (FOC 1, p. 106)
309) "Serenity" ("Serenity," 1:30)
310) "Ariel" ("The Message" DVD commentary, 26:31)
311) "The Train Job" (DVD feature "Here's How It Was," 3:45)
312) Book does not appear in "Ariel" ("Ariel," 1:29)
313) "Bushwhacked" (FOC 1, p. 84)
314) "Jaynestown" (FOC 2, p. 14)
315) "The Message" ("Re-Lighting the Firefly," *Serenity* DVD extra)
316) "Out of Gas" (FOC 2, p. 50)
317) "Out of Gas" ("Out of Gas" DVD commentary, 0:18)
318) "Objects in Space" ("Objects in Space," 7:59)
319) Whedon appears in "The Message" as a mourner at Tracey's funeral (http://www.xapz.com/xapz!/2009000100.htm)

CHAPTER 5

320) Alliance Short Range Enforcement Vessel (FOC 3, p. 131)
321) 03-K64 [zero three dash kay six four] ("The Train Job," 8:08)
322) "They fall right out of the sky" (*Serenity*, 30:04)
323) Vertical Take-Off & Landing (DVD feature "10th Character," 7:35)
324) The engine room ("The Train Job," 11:56)
325) The galley ("Bushwhacked," 11:19)
326) The Brutus ("Serenity," 18:30)

327) The primary buffer panel (*Serenity*, 10:29)
328) C deck ("Bushwhacked," 11:46)
329) Fast burn rocket shuttle ("War Stories," 18:24)
330) The pulse beacon (*Serenity*, 53:12)
331) Red ("Out of Gas," 33:00)
332) The Alliance Cruiser/the Dortmunder (FOC 3, p. 122)
333) The air ("Serenity," 7:25)
334) The engine room ("Our Mrs. Reynolds," 9:31)
335) Incense ("Out of Gas," 41:58)
336) Zoe and Simon (*Serenity*, 1:09:19)
337) a Trans-U ("Serenity," 53:05)
338) Forty thousand ("Bushwhacked," 27:14)
339) I.A.V. Dortmunder ("Serenity," 7:53)
340) Skull and crossbones (FOC 2, p. 29)
341) The D.C. line ("Bushwhacked," 23:01)
342) Magellan ("Safe," 24:56)
343) Standard radion-accelerator core ("The Train Job," 8:05)
344) True ("Serenity," 26:51)
345) A Crazy Ivan ("Serenity," 1:18:01)
346) Six ("Our Mrs. Reynolds," 36:51)
347) A Barn Swallow (*Serenity*, 23:00)
348) The plating ("Shindig," 24:40)
349) False. It's the port engine. ("Serenity," 1:18:46)
350) Seven (*Serenity*, 56:20)
351) Kaylee ("Ariel," 8:38)
352) The fifth car ("The Train Job," 15:54)
353) The fore-couple ("The Message," 28:25)
354) Two ("Bushwhacked," 42:58)
355) Override the standard guidance protocol ("Trash," 20:03)
356) One-quarter less than his asking price ("Out of Gas," 27:33)
357) Changes the ignition sequence ("War Stories," 11:53)
358) Zoe ("Out of Gas," 0:57)
359) "Smallish" ("Out of Gas," 26:09)
360) Wash ("The Train Job," 37:30)
361) Red ("Out of Gas," 29:53)
362) Zoe (*Serenity*, 20:28)

CHAPTER 6

363) Six years ("Serenity," 5:05)
364) About twelve years before (*Serenity*, 1:20:41)
365) Six years ("Trash," 25:21)
366) Zoe (*Serenity*, Alliance Database, Blu-ray Special Features)
367) An hour ("Ariel," 14:59)
368) Eleven years ("Safe," 0:10)
369) Juggling geese ("Our Mrs. Reynolds," 20:12)
370) Unification Day or U Day ("The Train Job," 1:28 & 5:22)
371) Eight months ("The Train Job," 18:02)
372) Twenty-six years old ("Jaynestown," 18:34)
373) Fourteen ("Serenity," 46:15)
374) Since they were on Ariel ("Objects in Space," 23:54)
375) Six months ("Jaynestown," 36:30)
376) Once a year ("Ariel," 1:52)
377) A couple of hours ("Out of Gas," 14:21)
378) It was on a warrant for his arrest ("Out of Gas," 7:08)
379) 500 years (SOC, p. 12)
380) Three weeks ("Safe," 6:07)
381) Three years ("The Train Job," 34:01)
382) Two days ("War Stories," 32:43)
383) Seven weeks (SOC, p. 14)
384) Five years (*Serenity*, Alliance Database, Blu-ray Special Features)
385) Kaylee (*Serenity*, Alliance Database, Blu-ray Special Features)
386) 8.6 seconds ("Safe," 3:30)
387) September 30, 2005 (www.boxofficemojo.com/movies/?id=serenity.htm)
388) Seventeen (*Serenity*, 13:05)
389) Eight months (*Serenity*, 37:57)
390) Another week ("Serenity," 43:26)
391) September 20, 2468 (*Serenity*, 36:34)
392) Having sex ("Out of Gas," 18:54)
393) Three ("Safe," 18:10)
394) An hour (*Serenity*, 53:37)
395) Two days ("War Stories" DVD commentary, 22:40)

396) Four years ("Jaynestown," 25:18)
397) Eight months ("Serenity," 45:03)
398) Twelve (SOC, p. 107)
399) October 14, 2489 (2489/10/14) (*Serenity*, Alliance Database, Blu-ray Special Features)
400) November (*Serenity*, Alliance Database, Blu-ray Special Features)
401) September (*Firefly* DVD box set)
402) Jewel Staite and Morena Baccarin were both born on June 2 (1982 and 1979, respectively; http://www.imdb.com/name/nm0821612/; http://www.imdb.com/name/nm1072555/)
403) Five to ten ("The Message," 15:55)

CHAPTER 7

404) She didn't haggle with them over the price ("Serenity," 1:03:12)
405) Hyman Roth from *The Godfather Part II* ("The Train Job" DVD commentary, 14:40)
406) One ("Ariel," 34:33)
407) Marco ("Out of Gas," 35:28)
408) Amnon the postmaster ("The Message," 16:49)
409) Pride (*Serenity*, 6:45)
410) How easily she took his gun out of his holster ("Trash," 35:18)
411) Petaline ("Heart of Gold," 38:00)
412) True ("War Stories," 24:58)
413) A mosquito bite ("Serenity," 39:22)
414) A whip ("War Stories," 2:03)
415) His right eye ("Jaynestown," 25:48)
416) Kaylee ("Objects in Space," 19:00)
417) Bridget ("Trash," 1:41)
418) Stitch Hessian ("Jaynestown," 34:37)
419) Punches him in the face ("Shindig," 25:24)
420) Hit him on the head ("Trash," 24:05)
421) Mal ("Objects in Space," 17:43)

422) A dozen ("Shindig," 26:19)
423) A Golden Retriever ("Objects in Space," 36:33)
424) True ("Shindig," 5:25)
425) Jubal Early (FOC 2, p. 186)
426) YoSafBridge ("Trash," 29:12)
427) Are you a lion? ("Objects in Space," 22:49)
428) Hats ("Serenity" DVD commentary, 8:45)
429) She will be his personal companion ("Shindig," 37:30)
430) A junker ("Bushwhacked," 30:30)
431) Twice ("Shindig," 38:23)
432) Red ("Objects in Space," 7:11)
433) A witch ("Safe," 35:26)
434) Lund (FOC 1, p. 54)
435) True ("Objects in Space," 18:07)
436) Five times (*Serenity*, 36:36)
437) A bounty hunter ("Objects in Space," 23:38)
438) True ("Heart of Gold," 11:23)
439) Crow ("The Train Job" DVD commentary, 14:50)
440) The ugly one ("Out of Gas," 35:07)
441) Inara ("Heart of Gold," 35:47)
442) Two-Fry ("Serenity," 1:10:42)
443) False ("Objects in Space," 17:43)
444) 200 Platinum ("Serenity," 1:08:23)
445) His left eye (*Serenity*, 1:46:48)
446) She was sold to slavers ("Trash," 25:34)
447) Adelai ("The Train Job," 13:59)
448) In his left leg ("Objects in Space," 39:10)
449) The right eye (*Serenity: Those Left Behind* graphic novel)
450) On his hand ("Ariel," 30:28)
451) False. It was five times as much ("War Stories," 26:03)
452) Simon ("Jaynestown," 31:58)
453) Laurence ("Serenity," 51:45)
454) Shadow puppets ("The Message," 21:54)
455) He's getting a haircut ("Shindig," 29:11)
456) The Operative (SOC, p. 21)
457) One tenth of a percent (*Serenity*, 1:19:13)
458) An ear ("Serenity," 52:08)
459) She kicks him in the head ("Our Mrs. Reynolds," 28:05)

460) He skimmed from a protection fund ("War Stories," 2:11)
461) Wash his feet ("Our Mrs. Reynolds," 14:21)
462) Two hundred thousand ("Objects in Space," 28:16)
463) He slides down the stairs and kicks Book in the head ("Objects in Space," 21:47)
464) Czech (FOC 1, p. 59)
465) Zoe could get naked ("Shindig," 31:10)
466) Her pinky ("Our Mrs. Reynolds," 27:30)
467) To be his personal companion ("Shindig," 24:00)
468) Yolanda ("Trash," 33:10)
469) Right ("Shindig," 36:45)
470) False ("War Stories," 27:16)
471) She was kidnapped ("Trash," 21:59)
472) Four ("War Stories," 22:57)
473) Arson ("Objects in Space," 34:53)
474) Six ("Serenity," 1:10:50)
475) In a cargo container ("Trash," 11:58)
476) Three (*Serenity*, 1:39:17)
477) Harken (FOC 1, p. 96)
478) Yes ("The Train Job," 15:38)
479) An albatross (*Serenity*, 51:50)
480) Yolanda ("Trash," 24:10)
481) She kicks him in the head ("Trash," 31:12)
482) Crow ("The Train Job," 14:02)
483) Lipstick ("Trash," 4:54)
484) Ath ("Shindig," 22:21)
485) Fresh bao ("Our Mrs. Reynolds," 13:19)
486) Five ("Out of Gas," 34:44)
487) Simon ("Objects in Space" DVD commentary, 19:14)
488) True ("Ariel," 33:25)
489) Kozick ("Heart of Gold," 31:53)
490) True ("Trash," 6:52)
491) Keeping them (the secrets) (*Serenity*, 7:35)
492) McGinnis ("Ariel," 29:11)
493) Three ("War Stories," 37:57)
494) His right shoulder (*Serenity*, 1:39:14)
495) From his nose ("Ariel," 33:13)
496) 800 square ("Trash," 25:01)

CHAPTER 8

497)   Fifteen percent ("Jaynestown," 11:47)
498)   River (*Serenity*, 1:17:58)
499)   Six ("Our Mrs. Reynolds," 16:41)
500)   Pascaline or Pascaline D ("The Train Job," 26:15)
501)   His hat ("The Message," 5:26)
502)   "Short interval" ("Serenity" DVD commentary, 15:08)
503)   Adrenaline ("Out of Gas," 13:06)
504)   A palm tree ("Serenity," 6:52)
505)   False ("Trash," 22:18)
506)   Mal ("Objects in Space," 4:58)
507)   The American flag and the Chinese flag ("The Train Job" DVD commentary, 23:05)
508)   From biggest to smallest, or "the next biggest one" ("Heart of Gold," 16:22)
509)   A meat grinder ("Safe," 3:07)
510)   False ("Objects in Space," 5:01)
511)   Kaylee ("The Message," 42:32)
512)   Milk and hay ("Safe," 10:58)
513)   A 3-D neuro-imager ("Ariel," 6:51)
514)   A grenade the size of a battery ("War Stories," 5:34)
515)   Zoe ("The Message," 12:49)
516)   Water, or a fire hose ("Heart of Gold," 33:48)
517)   The bag of money ("Safe," 14:51)
518)   A switchblade ("War Stories," 6:13)
519)   A cross ("Serenity,"1:48)
520)   Catalyzer on the port compression coil blew ("Out of Gas," 13:34)
521)   A tongue depressor ("Safe," 23:16)
522)   Hodgeberries ("Safe," 30:11)
523)   Fencing the Mona Lisa ("The Message," 3:14)
524)   A testicle ("Shindig," 10:29)
525)   It is made completely out of plastic (FOC 3, p. 44)
526)   A hanky ("Safe," 21:37)
527)   Wobbly-headed geisha dolls ("Trash," 11:02)
528)   Two ("Our Mrs. Reynolds," 0:19)
529)   A screwdriver (*Serenity*, 1:42:19)

530) "All the logs on behavioral modification triggers" (*Serenity*, 8:27)
531) Two ("Trash," 12:33)
532) Flour ("Out of Gas," 7:17)
533) False ("Jaynestown," 38:48)
534) Protein ("Out of Gas," 7:19)
535) True ("Heart of Gold," 11:50)
536) An ice planet ("The Message," 4:07)
537) False ("Ariel," 32:04)
538) His gun ("Objects in Space," 24:18)
539) True ("Trash," 37:35)
540) A swan ("Safe," 7:29)
541) 28 ("Out of Gas," 41:55; "War Stories," 18:12)
542) Flowers ("Trash," 18:42)
543) A wrench ("Ariel," 37:49)
544) The Lassiter ("The Message," 21:06)
545) His stomach ("Jaynestown," 1:13)
546) Small concealable weapons ("Heart of Gold," 3:03)
547) Cattle ("Shindig," 43:04)
548) One ("War Stories," 24:58)
549) A crate of apples ("War Stories," 4:53)
550) Jayne's ("Objects in Space," 7:51)
551) Jayne ("Jaynestown," 38:38)
552) A rabbit ("Safe," 4:20)
553) A rain stick ("Our Mrs. Reynolds," 2:32)
554) Tape ("Jaynestown," 0:53)
555) Chocolate ("Out of Gas," 7:27)
556) Horseshoes ("Ariel," 4:40)
557) A long-sleeved purple shirt ("Safe," 23:36)
558) A shot of calaphar (*Serenity*, 1:40:50)
559) Callahan fullbore autolock ("Our Mrs. Reynolds," 16:47)
560) Rub soup in our hair ("Objects in Space," 7:27)
561) A Bowie knife (FOC 2, p. 106)
562) A Tyrannosaurus Rex and a Stegosaurus ("Serenity," 6:22)
563) Nothing ("Out of Gas," 7:05)
564) A musical instrument ("Heart of Gold," 20:32)
565) Black market beagles ("Safe," 5:46)
566) Some money ("Safe," 23:28)

567) A stethoscope ("Safe," 23:16)
568) Check Battery ("Heart of Gold," 37:01)
569) Tall Card ("Shindig" DVD commentary, 16:06)
570) Telofonix ("Ariel," 16:48)
571) Red ("Shindig," 14:05)
572) A deck of cards ("Trash," 16:23)
573) White ("Our Mrs. Reynolds," 3:12)
574) A compression coil ("Serenity," 17:38)
575) Red ("Serenity," 41:20)
576) Cry Baby ("Serenity," 9:28)
577) Eliminating the middleman/sell direct to local doctors ("War Stories," 6:47)
578) Beans ("The Message," 8:25)
579) A catalyzer ("Out of Gas," 37:21)
580) Divert the nav sats to the transmitter ("Out of Gas," 17:43)
581) Reg couple ("Out of Gas," 20:17)
582) Apresaline ("Ariel," 20:07)
583) The original handheld laser pistol ("Trash," 12:30)
584) Adrenaline ("Out of Gas," 12:41)
585) A flash bomb (*Serenity*, 55:32)
586) G-23 Paxilon Hydroclorate (*Serenity*, 1:18:30)
587) A cow fetus ("The Message," 0:37)
588) They are poison ("Safe," 31:56)
589) Ancient Egyptians ("Jaynestown," 11:51)
590) A post holer ("Safe," 8:41)
591) A decorative plate ("Safe," 7:56)
592) 60,000 ("Jaynestown," 15:22)
593) Defibrillator paddles ("Ariel," 20:48)
594) Chinese Checkers ("The Train Job," 0:45)
595) Jayne Cobb ("Jaynestown," 6:14)
596) Management not responsible for ball failure ("Shindig," 0:28)
597) A piece of bread ("Safe," 41:50)
598) A shirt ("Ariel," 3:34)
599) 47 (FOC 1, p. 131)
600) Noah's Ark ("Jaynestown," 10:20)
601) Pink ("Jaynestown," 9:59)

602) A dedicated source box ("Safe," 1:29)
603) A stick ("Objects in Space," 4:34)
604) Through the air processors (*Serenity*, 1:18:30)
605) Fruity Oaty Bars (*Serenity*, 32:35)
606) A dermal mender ("War Stories," 39:36)
607) Slink ("Shindig," 7:10)

CHAPTER 9

608) Their belly buttons (*Serenity*, 17:19)
609) The statue of Jayne ("Jaynestown," 8:34)
610) (H) Understand (*Finding Serenity*, p. 231)
611) (F) Junk (*Finding Serenity*, p. 234)
612) (C) Dog crap (*Finding Serenity*, p. 232)
613) (A) Bastard (*Finding Serenity*, p. 230)
614) (D) Garbage (*Finding Serenity*, p. 232)
615) (G) Little sister (*Finding Serenity*, p. 232)
616) (E) Hello (*Finding Serenity*, p. 234)
617) (B) Butt (*Finding Serenity*, p. 231)
618) "I never married." ("Serenity," 18:36)
619) "I like this ship" ("Objects in Space," 19:04)
620) Kaylee ("Heart of Gold," 9:39)
621) Explode (*Serenity*, 10:55)
622) Saffron ("Our Mrs. Reynolds," 10:07)
623) Simon ("Objects in Space," 5:32)
624) "Hi" ("The Train Job," 17:28)
625) Lieutenant Womack ("The Message," 40:05)
626) "You find someone to carry you." ("The Message," 41:28)
627) "wear a shiny hat" ("Serenity," 17:42)
628) People who talk at the theater ("Our Mrs. Reynolds," 12:04)
629) Every dollar and leavin' five cents ("Jaynestown," 13:54)
630) Nandi ("Heart of Gold," 14:16)
631) Eta Kooram Nah Smech (SOC, p. 89)
632) "I like smacking 'em" ("Safe," 5:28)
633) Kaylee ("Ariel," 36:11)
634) "I will end you" ("Our Mrs. Reynolds," 1:13)

635) "It's okay to leave them to die" (*Serenity*, 15:52)

636) "Yep...That went well." ("Trash," 0:28)

637) Simon ("Out of Gas," 15:12)

638) Kneecaps ("War Stories," 32:00)

639) Zoe ("Safe," 39:31)

640) Tracey ("The Message," 35:05)

641) It's manly and impulsive ("The Train Job," 11:44)

642) Rosemary ("Serenity," 31:51)

643) His intimidating manner ("The Message," 4:15)

644) Corpsified and gross ("Shindig," 18:44)

645) River ("Jaynestown," 40:30)

646) Dying for his beliefs (*Serenity*, 1:37:50)

647) "Oh God, oh God, we're all gonna die" (*Serenity*, 10:50)

648) Armed ("Serenity," 1:24:51)

649) River finding Jayne's gun ("Objects in Space," 5:06)

650) "Someone who gets other people killed" (*Serenity*, 18:25)

651) Jayne ("Ariel," 40:50)

652) True ("Heart of Gold," 6:12)

653) Naked ("Trash," 34:33)

654) Book ("War Stories," 0:53)

655) Space ("Objects in Space," 16:08)

656) "We'd all be eatin' steak" ("Objects in Space," 14:03)

657) The end scene when Mal tells Jayne, "You do it to any of my people, you do it to me!" (FOC 2, p. 83)

658) In "War Stories" when Simon unwraps Mal's ear that Niska has cut off ("War Stories" DVD commentary, 29:20)

659) Wash ("Heart of Gold," 16:43)

660) Simon ("War Stories," 1:33)

661) Kaylee ("Out of Gas," 19:45)

662) Kaylee ("Jaynestown," 8:39)

663) Malcolm Reynolds' widow ("Our Mrs. Reynolds," 30:29)

664) "He looks better in red" ("Ariel," 2:32)

665) Mr. Universe (*Serenity*, 40:18)

666) Cortical electrodes ("Ariel," 15:27)

667) Jayne ("Serenity," 51:17)

668) "Jayne" ("Jaynestown," 15:37)

669) Mal ("Out of Gas," 29:32)
670) Not to tell the other what he did ("Ariel," 40:33)
671) The "alien" in the tank from "The Message" ("The Message," 2:31)
672) Hilarious ("The Train Job," 8:26)
673) "No power in the 'verse can stop me" ("War Stories," 38:12)
674) Kaylee and River ("War Stories," 4:48)
675) "Well, Jayne ain't a girl!" ("Trash," 16:03)
676) Jubal Early ("Objects in Space," 27:18)
677) Kaylee ("Shindig," 14:58)
678) Jubal Early's "Well, here I am" ("Objects in Space" DVD commentary, 43:07)
679) River ("The Message," 12:23)
680) The "alien" in the tank from "The Message" ("The Message," 2:57)
681) A pony and a plastic rocket (*Serenity*, 50:43)
682) Comprehend ("Objects in Space," 5:06)
683) Jayne ("The Train Job," 22:00)
684) "Is it Christmas?" ("Our Mrs. Reynolds," 31:47)
685) Wash ("The Message," 27:40)
686) Zoe ("Our Mrs. Reynolds," 6:54)
687) Shepherd Book (*Serenity*, 1:22:01)
688) "It's a chain I beat you with 'til you understand who's in ruttin' command here." ("The Train Job," 32:11)
689) His arm ("Heart of Gold," 10:49)
690) "Well, here I am." ("Objects in Space," 43:11)
691) Middle ("Our Mrs. Reynolds," 17:21)
692) The Operative (*Serenity*, 53:06)
693) "It was the best day ever." ("Safe," 23:21)
694) They are the only ones who don't think the situation is funny ("Our Mrs. Reynolds," 9:13)
695) "I really don't." (*Serenity*, 34:45)
696) Bester ("Out of Gas," 12:12)
697) (1) In a fair fight, (2) if someone is gonna start a fair fight, (3) if someone bothers him, (4) if there's a woman, or (5) if he's getting paid (*Serenity*, 27:44)
698) Jayne ("Trash," 41:05)

CHAPTER 10

699) Juilliard (FOC 1, p. 68)
700) Adam Baldwin (FOC 2, p. 106)
701) (F) Tim Minear (FOC 1, p. 84)
702) (C) Jane Espenson (FOC 1, p. 106)
703) (D) Drew Z. Greenberg (FOC 1, p. 126)
704) (H) Joss Whedon (FOC 1, p. 156)
705) (B) Ben Edlund (FOC 2, p. 14)
706) (G) Jose Molina (FOC 2, p. 62)
707) (A) Cheryl Cain (FOC 2, p. 86)
708) (E) Brett Matthews (FOC 2, p. 160)
709) "Heart of Gold" (FOC 2, p. 161)
710) Nathan Fillion (DVD feature "Here's How It Was," 8:50)
711) Alan Tudyk and Ron Glass (http://www.imdb.com/title/tt0795368/; http://www.imdb.com/title/tt1321509/)
712) Joss Whedon ("Serenity," 12:50)
713) Alan Tudyk ("The Message" DVD commentary, 20:00)
714) Adam Baldwin's kids (*Serenity* Collector's Edition DVD Commentary, 1:25)
715) True ("Our Mrs. Reynolds" Blu-ray commentary, 9:14)
716) Morena Baccarin (FOC 3, p. 65)
717) The Tick (FOC 2, p. 14)
718) Warren Oates (from *The Wild Bunch*) and Eli Wallach (from *The Good, The Bad, and The Ugly*) (DVD feature "Here's How It Was," 9:47)
719) Simon's (FOC 1, p. 127)
720) Joss Whedon (FOC 1, p. 142)
721) Greg Edmonson ("Serenity," 12:46)
722) Alan Tudyk ("Serenity" DVD commentary, 7:07)
723) *Serenity* (http://www.imdb.com/name/nm0117989/)
724) Both (http://www.imdb.com/name/nm0172837/)
725) *Firefly* (http://www.imdb.com/name/nm0249557/)
726) Both (http://www.imdb.com/name/nm0489809/)
727) *Serenity* (http://www.imdb.com/name/nm0578814/)
728) *Firefly* (http://www.imdb.com/name/nm0591101/)
729) Both (http://www.imdb.com/name/nm0003398/)

730) *Firefly* (http://www.imdb.com/name/nm0495348/)
731) Nod and say, "Captain." (FOC 2, p. 61)
732) Nathan Fillion (FOC 2, p. 145)
733) *Nausea* by Jean-Paul Sartre ("Objects in Space" DVD commentary, 8:54)
734) Brett Matthews (FOC 2, p. 160)
735) Doug Savant ("Bushwhacked," 4:03)
736) Jane Espenson (FOC 1, p. 106)
737) *The Searchers* (1956) (FOC 2, p. 84)
738) Shepherd Book (FOC 2, p. 22)
739) (B) Fanty (http://www.imdb.com/name/nm0271096/)
740) (D) Mingo (http://www.imdb.com/name/nm0271134/)
741) (H) Young boy at Haven (http://www.imdb.com/name/nm1782585/)
742) (A) Dr. Mathias (http://www.imdb.com/name/nm0386871/)
743) (F) Reaver victim (http://www.imdb.com/name/nm1097351/)
744) (E) Mr. Universe (http://www.imdb.com/name/nm0472710/)
745) (C) Lenore (http://www.imdb.com/name/nm0741592/)
746) (G) River's teacher (http://www.imdb.com/name/nm0853231/)
747) *The Killer Angels* by Michael Shaara (SOC, p. 8)
748) Ron Glass (http://www.imdb.com/name/nm0322002/)
749) Adam Baldwin (DVD feature "Here's How It Was," 14:55)
750) Zac Efron as Young Simon in "Safe" ("Safe," 42:08)
751) (A) Edward Atterton (http://www.imdb.com/name/nm0041029/)
752) (H) Mark Sheppard (http://www.imdb.com/name/nm0791968/)
753) (G) Carlos Jacott (http://www.imdb.com/name/nm0415070/)
754) (C) Richard Brooks (http://www.imdb.com/name/nm1444462/)
755) (D) Melinda Clarke (http://www.imdb.com/name/nm0164918/)

756) (E) Michael Fairman
(http://www.imdb.com/name/nm0265637/)

757) (B) Bonnie Bartlett
(http://www.imdb.com/name/nm0058783/)

758) (F) Christina Hendricks
(http://www.imdb.com/name/nm0376716/)

759) (I) Jonathan M. Woodward
(http://www.imdb.com/name/nm0940950/)

760) Nathan Fillion and Adam Baldwin (FOC 3, p. 50)

761) *C.S.I.: Crime Scene Investigation* (FOC 2, p. 167)

762) Nathan Fillion ("Re-Lighting the Firefly," *Serenity* DVD extra, 4:46)

763) Three ("Serenity," "The Train Job," and "Objects in Space") (http://www.imdb.com/name/nm0923736/)

764) Ben Edlund (FOC 2, p. 14)

765) Pink flamingoes ("Shindig" DVD commentary, 9:20)

766) False. He is a Buddhist ("Out of Gas" DVD commentary, 16:17)

767) Sonny Rhodes ("Serenity," 12:50)

768) (F) Carey Meyer
(http://www.imdb.com/name/nm0583047/)

769) (G) Loni Peristere
(http://www.imdb.com/name/nm0003398/)

770) (B) Nick Brandon
(http://www.imdb.com/name/nm0104790/)

771) (I) Peter M. Robarts
(http://www.imdb.com/name/nm0730179/)

772) (A) David Boyd
(http://www.imdb.com/name/nm0101741/)

773) (E) Jenny Lynn
(http://www.imdb.com/name/nm0528709/)

774) (C) Mark Cleary
(http://www.imdb.com/name/nm0165860/)

775) (H) Ron Pipes
(http://www.imdb.com/name/nm0684962/)

776) (D) David A. Koneff
(http://www.imdb.com/name/nm0465004/)

777) False. She videotaped her first audition and sent it in (FOC 1, p. 114)
778) Book (FOC 2, p. 146)
779) Jayne (FOC 2, p. 170)
780) (E) Michael Grossman (FOC 1, p. 126)
781) (B) Vondie Curtis Hall (FOC 1, p. 156)
782) (D) Marita Grabiak (FOC 2, p. 14)
783) (H) David Solomon (FOC 2, p. 40)
784) (F) Allan Kroeker (FOC 2, p. 62)
785) (A) James Contner (FOC 2, p. 86)
786) (C) Vern Gillum (FOC 2, p. 114)
787) (G) Tim Minear (FOC 2, p. 138)
788) (I) Thomas J. Wright (FOC 2, p. 160)
789) He is director Marita Grabiak's son (Marita Grabiak personal interview)
790) Jewel Staite (Born June 2, 1982; http://www.imdb.com/name/nm0821612/)
791) "fighting elves" (FOC 2, p. 15)
792) Three: Nathan Fillion (Canada), Jewel Staite (Canada) and Morena Baccarin (Brazil) (http://www.imdb.com/title/tt0303461/)
793) Four (Andy Umberger, Carlos Jacott, Jeff Ricketts, and Jonathan M. Woodward) (FOC 1, p. 13)
794) Gina Torres and Morena Baccarin (http://www.gina-torres.com/about/; http://www.tv.com/people/morena-baccarin/)

CHAPTER 11

795) Her history of how she came to be on the ship (with a fake name) ("Shindig" DVD commentary, 32:13)
796) Joss Whedon's (FOC 2, p. 58)
797) *The Tempest* (*Serenity* DVD commentary, 58:20)
798) The Vulcan salute from Star Trek (or "The Spock sign" as Alan Tudyk calls it) ("The Message" DVD commentary, 3:05)
799) Calvinball (FOC 1, p. 84)

800) Pretending to be electrocuted in "War Stories" (FOC 3, p. 48)

801) His wife, Kai Cole (SOC, p. 11)

802) Red and gold (DVD feature "10th Character," 2:46)

803) Was shot down after one sortie and was in prison for the rest of the war ("War Stories" DVD commentary, 6:00)

804) An old boyfriend of Joss Whedon's friend, "Brooke the chef" ("Serenity" DVD commentary, 1:10:42)

805) Gina Torres ("The Message" DVD commentary, 18:37)

806) Gina Torres was getting married and going on her honeymoon ("Out of Gas" DVD commentary, 9:55)

807) False (*Serenity* DVD commentary, 1:30:44)

808) Twenty pounds (FOC 2, p. 146)

809) Mal (SOC, p. 11)

810) Simon ("Shindig" DVD commentary, 14:08)

811) The Alliance Cruiser/I.A.V Dortmunder ("Serenity" DVD commentary, 7:57)

812) True (FOC 1, p. 72)

813) True ("War Stories" DVD commentary, 0:20)

814) Charles Ingalls (Pa on *Little House on the Prairie*) (FOC 2, p. 117)

815) The opening theme song ("Objects in Space" DVD commentary, 6:15)

816) Wash ("Our Mrs. Reynolds" Blu-ray commentary, 28:20)

817) Hooks hanging from the ceiling ("War Stories" DVD commentary, 19:45)

818) Kelly Freas ("Our Mrs. Reynolds" Blu-ray commentary, 1:00)

819) Mr. Universe (*Serenity* DVD commentary, 1:23:16)

820) Tiffany & Co. ("War Stories" DVD commentary, 25:46)

821) River wanted to marry Simon ("Our Mrs. Reynolds" Blu-ray commentary, 33:25)

822) Inara and Mal walking through a wooded, pastoral scene ("Shindig" DVD commentary, 00:50)

823) Harry Dean Stanton's character Brett from *Alien* (FOC 2, p. 92)

824) "The Message" (FOC 2, p. 153)

825) Nathan Fillion ("*Firefly* Reunion" Blu-ray feature, 4:30)

826) Serenity (the ship) (DVD feature "10th Character," 1:00)
827) Carlos Jacott (Dobson in "Serenity") (FOC 1, p. 60)
828) Alan Tudyk (*Serenity* DVD Outtakes, 2:35)
829) Dressing the 350 extras as mudders in "Jaynestown" (FOC 2, p. 30)
830) Nathan Fillion's (FOC 2, p. 83)
831) Adam Baldwin (FOC 1, p. 165)
832) It looks like a woman's sweater ("The Message" DVD commentary, 42:05)
833) Dealing with uncomfortable costumes (FOC 2, p. 50)
834) Drums (FOC 1, p. 110)
835) Adam Baldwin (FOC 1, p. 32)
836) 300 ("Shindig" DVD commentary, 11:00)
837) Summer Glau (FOC 1, p. 71)
838) The mall (where they receive Tracey's body) in "The Message" (FOC 1, p. 12)
839) Jeannie's bottle from *I Dream of Jeannie* ("Serenity" DVD commentary, 1:21:50)
840) Joss Whedon (FOC 2, p. 115)
841) Summer Glau's ("Shindig" DVD commentary, 2:59)
842) When Mal first sees Serenity in "Out of Gas" (FOC 2, p. 47)
843) Costume designer Shawna Trpcic's ("Shindig" DVD commentary, 11:18)
844) Alan Tudyk's ("Out of Gas" DVD commentary, 11:35)
845) Jubal Early threatening Kaylee in "Objects in Space" ("Objects in Space" DVD commentary, 18:34)
846) Five (SOC, p. 10)
847) Jubal Early's (FOC 2, p. 197)
848) Three ("Serenity" DVD commentary, 36:00)
849) Boba Fett ("Objects in Space" DVD commentary, 3:30)
850) False (*Serenity* Collector's Edition DVD commentary, 49:50)
851) The Chinese ("Serenity" DVD commentary, 7:25)
852) Gina Torres (to Laurence Fishburne) ("Out of Gas" DVD commentary, 9:55)
853) *Sgt. Pepper's Lonely Hearts Club Band* (FOC 2, p. 115)
854) None (FOC 2, p. 9)

855) Book's bible (*"Firefly* Reunion" Blu-ray commentary, 15:50)

856) The head of Jayne's statue (FOC 2, p. 18)

857) Jayne ("The Train Job" DVD commentary, 32:20)

858) *Firefly's* first Christmas party (DVD feature "Gag Reel," 0:01)

859) Kaylee eating the strawberry (FOC 1, p. 6)

860) Han Solo in carbonite (FOC 2, p. 145)

861) True (FOC 1, p. 6)

862) The "Space Bazaar" (where the crew picks up Tracey's body) in "The Message" (FOC 3, p. 128)

863) They would end up getting engaged and married ("Shindig" DVD commentary, 14:55)

864) A chocolate doughnut and Dr. Pepper (*Serenity* Collector's Edition DVD commentary, 47:40)

865) Hanging from wires ("Serenity" DVD commentary, 5:31)

866) Playing Xbox ("Serenity" DVD commentary, 1:16:55)

867) Nathan Fillion (FOC 1, p. 36)

868) The Blue-Gloved men (FOC 2, p. 80)

869) Harrison Ford ("A Filmmaker's Journey," *Serenity* Collector's Edition DVD extra)

870) Mal telling Simon in the cargo bay that Kaylee is dead ("Serenity" DVD commentary, 1:00:20)

871) True ("The Message" DVD commentary, 3:17)

872) The name. The ship was then designed around the Firefly name ("Serenity" DVD commentary, 41:27)

873) Loni Peristere (FOC 2, p. 185)

874) The orgasm scene in "Serenity" (FOC 1, p. 32)

875) It was supposed to be inserted upside down, but wasn't ("The Message" DVD commentary, 0:43)

876) Summer Glau (FOC 3, p. 31)

877) The cargo bay doors should go in the back for aerodynamics (FOC 1, p. 11)

878) The Reavers and the Alliance (FOC 1, p. 84)

879) Badger ("Serenity" DVD commentary, 19:12)

880) Adam Baldwin ("War Stories" DVD commentary, 36:10)

881) Mr. Universe (*Serenity* DVD commentary, 39:55)

882) "Objects in Space" (FOC 2, p. 205)

883) *Gone with the Wind* (1939) (FOC 1, p. 111)
884) Jayne ("Serenity" DVD commentary, 50:25)
885) Two days ("The Train Job" DVD commentary, 00:50)
886) The network wanted Mal to be more likable (FOC 1, p. 54)
887) Nathan Fillion (FOC 2, p. 96)
888) Joss Whedon's friend, *Toy Story* director John Lasseter (FOC 3, p. 40)
889) His niece (*Serenity* Collector's Edition DVD commentary, 45:07)
890) Joss Whedon's ("Shindig" DVD commentary, 31:19)
891) *The King & I* (1956) ("Shindig" DVD commentary, 14:40)
892) When all nine characters were around the dining room table (DVD feature "10th Character," 2:29)
893) A stuntman who was being flipped over the bar ("Shindig" DVD commentary, 2:05)
894) False. Eriksen bought them in the downtown LA toy district (FOC 1, p. 18)
895) True (FOC 2, p. 141)
896) None (FOC 2, p. 105)
897) Her marriage bond to Wash ("Shindig" DVD commentary, 3:21)
898) Mark Sheppard (FOC 1, p. 110)
899) Rebecca Gayheart ("Serenity" DVD commentary, 18:35)
900) Mary Parent ("Re-Lighting the Firefly," *Serenity* DVD extra)
901) Earrings (FOC 2, p. 48)
902) A Confederate general during the Civil War (http://www.history.com/topics/jubal-a-early)
903) False (FOC 1, p. 10)
904) Bending over Kaylee after she has been shot by Dobson in "Serenity" ("Serenity" DVD commentary, 39:43)
905) False. She was naked. (FOC 1, p. 37)
906) "Laughter for Chickens" or figuratively, "This is absurd" (*Serenity* Collector's Edition DVD commentary, 35:55)
907) The cargo bay of the ghost ship from "Bushwhacked" ("The Train Job" DVD commentary, 35:01)

908) Three (FOC 1, p. 82)

909) Joss Whedon (FOC 2, p. 192)

910) Mal's holster and gun belt (FOC 2, p. 116)

911) Kaylee (FOC 1, p. 150)

912) False. He says it took him two or three times hearing it to "get on board with it." ("War Stories" DVD commentary, 3:22)

913) Saffron ("Our Mrs. Reynolds" Blu-ray commentary, 26:00)

914) Inara (DVD feature "Here's How It Was," 9:15)

915) Kaylee being shot by Dobson ("Serenity" DVD commentary, 40:10)

916) Summer's feet ("Objects in Space" DVD commentary, 1:37)

917) Alan Tudyk ("Out of Gas" DVD commentary, 30:20)

CHAPTER 12

918) Jewel Staite (FOC 3, p. 138)

919) California Browncoats (http://www.californiabrowncoats.org/?p=90)

920) (F) Black Canary (http://www.imdb.com/name/nm1072555/)

921) (C) Superman (http://www.imdb.com/name/nm0000284/)

922) (A) Vigilante (http://www.imdb.com/name/nm0277213/)

923) (D) Supergirl (http://www.imdb.com/name/nm1132359/)

924) (B) Superwoman (http://www.imdb.com/name/nm0868659/)

925) (E) Green Arrow (http://www.imdb.com/name/nm0876138/)

926) The Ariel Ambulance Rescue Group (FOC 2, p. 68)

927) Inara (FOC 2, p. 124)

928) $4,700 ($4,707.57; http://www.californiabrowncoats.org/?p=90)

929) The Jetwash (*Serenity: Float Out*)
930) Adam Baldwin, Michael Fairman, Yan Feldman, and Raphael Feldman (http://browncoatsmovie.com/?page_id=425)
931) Nathan Fillion (*Entertainment Weekly*, March 25, 2011, p. 44)
932) Henry Evans (*Serenity: The Shepherd's Tale* graphic novel)
933) Kaylee (FOC 2, p.11)
934) Kerry Pearson (aka Lux Lucre) (http://www.fireflyfans.net/mthread.asp?b=7&t=3347)
935) On one of Jayne's t-shirts (FOC 1, p. 120)
936) Sean Maher and Jewel Staite (http://www.imdb.com/title/tt1665404/)
937) The Green Lantern logo (*Entertainment Weekly*, March 25, 2011)
938) The Marine Corps - Law Enforcement Foundation (http://www.californiabrowncoats.org/?p=90)
939) The Backup Bash (or the Browncoat Backup Bash) (FOC 2, p. 60)
940) Two (Summer Glau and Alan Tudyk) (http://www.imdb.com/title/tt1135300/)
941) Adam Baldwin, Summer Glau, and Gina Torres (http://www.imdb.com/title/tt0162065/)
942) Steven Swanson (FOC 3, p. 136)
943) One (Nathan Fillion) (http://www.imdb.com/title/tt0118276/)
944) One of his eyes (Serenity: *The Shepherd's Tale* graphic novel)
945) (B) John Cassaday (*Serenity: Those Left Behind* hardcover graphic novel)
946) E) Bryan Hitch (*Serenity: Those Left Behind* hardcover graphic novel)
947) (F) J. G. Jones (*Serenity: Those Left Behind* hardcover graphic novel)
948) (A) Tim Bradstreet (*Serenity: Those Left Behind* hardcover graphic novel)
949) (C) Jo Chen (*Serenity: Those Left Behind* hardcover graphic novel)

950) (I) Joe Quesada (*Serenity: Those Left Behind* hardcover graphic novel)

951) (H) Sean Phillips (*Serenity: Those Left Behind* hardcover graphic novel)

952) (D) Leinil Francis Yu (*Serenity: Those Left Behind* hardcover graphic novel)

953) (G) Joshua Middleton (*Serenity: Those Left Behind* hardcover graphic novel)

954) The Blue Sun Corporation (FOC 1, p. 13)

955) The *Firefly* Immediate Assistance program (FOC 2, p. 60)

956) Jane Espenson (*Finding Serenity & Serenity Found*)

957) "The Rime of the Ancient Mariner" (*Serenity*, 51:58; poem by Samuel Taylor Coleridge in *Lyrical Ballads*, 1798)

958) Agent Dobson (*Serenity: Those Left Behind* graphic novel)

959) The Civil War (http://www.history.com/topics/jubal-a-early)

960) Ron Glass (FOC 3, p. 138)

961) Kids Need to Read (http://www.kidsneedtoread.org/)

962) Jubal Early (http://www.moviesonline.ca/movienews_6536.html)

963) Adam Baldwin (*Serenity: Better Days* graphic novel)

964) Mojave, CA (FOC 2, p. 68)

965) *Mad Men* (http://www.imdb.com/name/nm0376716/)

966) Summer Glau (http://www.imdb.com/name/nm1132359/)

967) (H) Chloe (*How I Met Your Mother*) (http://www.imdb.com/name/nm1072555/)

968) (C) Special Agent Kenton (*Bones*) (http://www.imdb.com/name/nm0000284/)

969) (G) Kevin Callis (*Lost*) (http://www.imdb.com/name/nm0277213/)

970) (E) District Attorney Ford (*Dirty Sexy Money*) (http://www.imdb.com/name/nm0322002/)

971) (D) Him/herself (*The Big Bang Theory*) (http://www.imdb.com/name/nm1132359/)

972) (A) Conor Donovan (*Ghost Whisperer*) (http://www.imdb.com/name/nm0536883/)

973) (B) Dr. Keller (*Stargate: Atlantis*) (http://www.imdb.com/name/nm0821612/)

974) (I) Bree (*The Vampire Diaries*)
(http://www.imdb.com/name/nm0868659/)

975) (F) Dale Maddox (*V*)
(http://www.imdb.com/name/nm0876138/)

976) Zoe (*Serenity: Float Out*)

977) The end of the second season (FOC 2, p. 11)

978) Patton Oswalt (*Serenity: Float Out*)

979) *Serenity: Those Left Behind* (*Serenity: Those Left Behind* graphic novel)

980) Adam Baldwin and Jewel Staite (FOC 3, p. 144)

981) *Mosquito* (http://www.mosquitoverse.com/)

982) Keith R.A. DeCandido (SOC, p. 159)

983) "Dead or Alive"
(http://www.whedon.info/article.php3?id_article=8136)

984) Kaylee (FOC 2, p. 136)

985) *Community* (2x16 "Intermediate Documentary Filmmaking," 5:17)

986) Inkworks (www.inkworks.com)

987) *Variety* (December 9, 2002, volume 389, issue 4)

988) Gunnery Sgt. Buck
(http://www.imdb.com/name/nm0277213/)

989) *The Big Bang Theory* (3x22 "The Staircase Implementation" 7:47)

990) *Browncoats: Redemption* (FOC 3, p. 145)

991) Quantum Mechanix (aka QMx) (FOC 3, p. 140)

992) Nathan Fillion (*Serenity: Those Left Behind* graphic novel)

993) Nathan Fillion (*Serenity Found*, p. 49)

994) Four (http://www.imdb.com/title/tt0275137/)

995) Sean Maher
(http://seanmaher.info/excl20091206interview.html)

996) Summer Glau (2011) and Adam Baldwin (1996-1997)
(http://www.imdb.com/title/tt1593823/,
http://www.imdb.com/title/tt0115126/)

CHAPTER 13

997) (D) Fourth ("Serenity," 11:21)
998) (E) Fifth ("Serenity," 11:25)
999) (A) First ("Serenity," 11:05)
1000) (I) Ninth ("Serenity," 11:42)
1001) (H) Eighth ("Serenity," 11:38)
1002) (G) Seventh ("Serenity," 11:34)
1003) (F) Sixth ("Serenity," 11:28)
1004) (B) Second ("Serenity," 11:12)
1005) (C) Third ("Serenity," 11:17)
1006) Zoic (DVD feature "10th Character," 5:25)
1007) *Showtime* (2002) (FOC 2, p. 110)
1008) "Trash," "The Message," and "Heart of Gold" (*Firefly* DVD box set)
1009) A Taurus 85 revolver (FOC 1, p. 78)
1010) A rechargeable flashlight (FOC 3, p. 40)
1011) A Winchester rifle (FOC 1, p. 104)
1012) Visual effects supervisor Loni Peristere (FOC 3, p. 120)
1013) *The 6th Day* (2000) (FOC 3, p. 30)
1014) Joss Whedon (DVD feature "Joss Tours the Set")
1015) River (*Firefly* DVD Deleted Scenes, 0:46)
1016) False. All the cows were CGI ("Shindig" DVD commentary, 43:07)
1017) River's boots (FOC 1, p. 128)
1018) Mal coming out of his quarters on the ladder in "Serenity" (FOC 1, p. 14)
1019) Color reversal film ("Out of Gas" DVD commentary, 1:33)
1020) A sound effect ("somewhere between a chime and a tone") used to replace the traditional beeps heard on spaceships (FOC 2, p. 109)
1021) Major League Baseball playoffs (FOC 3, p. 29)
1022) $39 million ($38,869,464; www.boxofficemojo.com/movies/?id=serenity.htm)
1023) "Serenity," "Our Mrs. Reynolds," and "Objects in Space" (*Firefly* DVD Deleted Scenes)
1024) More actors' auditions than just his ("*Firefly* Reunion" Blu-ray feature, 2:40)

1025) Serenity crashing at Mr. Universe's complex (*Serenity* DVD commentary, 1:29:22)

1026) *Soldier* (1998) (FOC 1, p. 100)

1027) *The One* (2001) (FOC 2, p. 112)

1028) Shotgun blanks would have destroyed the space suit (FOC 2, p. 111)

1029) Mal, Book, Jayne, and Zoe (*Firefly* DVD box set)

1030) *Star Wars: Episode II – Attack of the Clones* ("The Train Job" DVD commentary, 13:50)

1031) *The Adventures of Brisco County Jr.* (FOC 1, p. 104)

1032) Deerskin (FOC 1, p. 82)

1033) Eight (FOC 3, p. 30)

1034) Joss Whedon (DVD feature "Joss Sings the *Firefly* Theme")

1035) "Our Mrs. Reynolds" ("Our Mrs. Reynolds," Blu-ray commentary)

1036) GBB Custom Gunleather (FOC 1, p. 81)

1037) Jayne's gun Vera (FOC 2, p. 110)

1038) Adam Baldwin singing "The Hero of Canton" (DVD Special Features, Disc 4)

1039) Mr. Sparkle (*Serenity*, Special Feature, 0:51)

1040) Miranda (*Serenity* DVD commentary, 1:14:31)

1041) Yes ("Serenity," 11:05 & *Serenity*, 10:27)

1042) Sean Maher's (DVD feature "Gag Reel," 0:48)

1043) False (FOC 2, p. 159)

1044) *The Limey* (1999) (FOC 1, p. 9)

1045) *Waterworld* (1995) (FOC 2, p. 30)

1046) Applied Effects (FOC 1, p. 78)

1047) Jayne's pistol (FOC 2, p. 112)

1048) 2007 (http://www.amazon.com/Serenity-Collectors-Nathan-Fillion/dp/B000Q9IZ5C)

1049) A feature on the Fruity Oaty Bars commercial (*Serenity*, Special Feature)

1050) Outstanding Special Visual Effects for a Series (http://www.imdb.com/title/tt0303461/awards)

Lightning Source UK Ltd.
Milton Keynes UK
UKHW01f0632110918
328670UK00004B/306/P